GREATER THAN
GOLD

GREATER THAN
GOLD

FROM ——— OLYMPIC HEARTBREAK —— TO ——— ULTIMATE REDEMPTION

DAVID BOUDIA

WITH TIM ELLSWORTH

NELSON
BOOKS

An Imprint of Thomas Nelson

Published in Nashville, Tennessee, by Nelson Books, an imprint of Thomas Nelson. Nelson Books and Thomas Nelson are registered trademarks of HarperCollins Christian Publishing, Inc.

Published in association with the literary agency of Shade Global and Wolgemuth & Associates, Inc.

Thomas Nelson titles may be purchased in bulk for educational, business, fund-raising, or sales promotional use. For information, please e-mail SpecialMarkets@ ThomasNelson.com.

Any Internet addresses, phone numbers, or company or product information printed in this book are offered as a resource and are not intended in any way to be or to imply an endorsement by Thomas Nelson, nor does Thomas Nelson vouch for the existence, content, or services of these sites, phone numbers, companies, or products beyond the life of this book.

Unless otherwise noted, Scripture quotations are taken from the ESV® Bible (The Holy Bible, English Standard Version®), copyright © 2001 by Crossway, a publishing ministry of Good News Publishers. Used by permission. All rights reserved.

Scripture quotations marked NIV are taken from the Holy Bible, New International Version®, NIV®. Copyright © 1973, 1978, 1984, 2011 by Biblica, Inc.™ Used by permission of Zondervan. All rights reserved worldwide. www.zondervan.com. The "NIV"and "New International Version" are trademarks registered in the United States Patent and Trademark Office by Biblica, Inc.™

Unless otherwise noted, insert photos are courtesy of the Boudia family.

ISBN-13: 978-0-7180-7879-9 (e-book)

Library of Congress Cataloging-in-Publication Data

Names: Boudia, David, 1989- I Ellsworth, Tim.
Title: Greater than Gold : from Olympic heartbreak to ultimate redemption /
    David Boudia with Tim Ellsworth.
Description: Nashville, Tennessee : Nelson Books, [2016]
Identifiers: LCCN 2015047778I ISBN 9780718077419 (HC) I ISBN 9780718078799
    (e-book)
Subjects: LCSH: Boudia, David, 1989- I Divers--United States--Biography. I
    Divers--Conduct of life.
Classification: LCC GV838.B68 A3 2016 I DDC 797.2/3092 [B] --dc23 LC record
available at https://lccn.loc.gov/2015047778

Printed in the United States of America

16 17 18 19 20 RRD 6 5 4 3 2 1

CONTENTS

INTRODUCTION

The important thing in life is not the triumph, but the fight; the essential thing is not to have won, but to have fought well.

—OLYMPIC CREED

As I stood on the 10-meter platform in Beijing in 2008, preparing for my final dive in the aqua-colored, puffy-looking Water Cube (the venue for all the aquatic events), I wanted to savor the moment. This was the pinnacle of athletic accomplishment for hundreds of athletes like me who had sweated, pushed, lifted, trained, sacrificed, and willed their way to the Olympics.

For me, that Olympic experience amounted to a whopping total of about 8.5 seconds in my individual event. The final in the 10-meter platform competition consists of six dives. A dive takes about 1.4 seconds. That means I spent roughly five hours a day, six days a week, three hundred days a year training and preparing for those 8.5 seconds. Plus, the fact that millions of people around the world were watching me as I stood there in a skimpy suit added to my drive to attain perfection. Talk about pressure.

My Olympic journey had been an all-consuming passion and obsession since I was seven years old. That was the start of my pursuit of the American dream—my belief that I could achieve riches, fame, and success. For me, the Olympics were my vehicle of choice to get the goods. The desire accelerated over time. Once I made the Olympics, just making it there was no longer enough. I wanted to win a medal. Then winning a medal wasn't enough. I wanted to win gold.

With a singular focus that never wavered, I pursued this dream of Olympic glory not for some noble purpose but because of what I thought it could deliver. My only desire in life was to please myself and do everything I could to make my life better, and I believed a gold medal would achieve that. A gold medal would mean fame and adoration. A gold medal would mean success. It would mean acceptance. It would mean happiness and joy.

So, relentlessly and doggedly, that's what I chased. And the harder I pressed and the closer I got to that goal, the more miserable life became. Every time I thought I had almost achieved the goal, suddenly a new one took its place. No matter what I accomplished and no matter how happy I should have been, fulfillment always seemed just beyond my grasp.

Sound familiar?

Maybe everyone else in your life thinks you have it all together, but you know better. You look in the mirror and you see the emptiness staring back at you that eludes everyone else. Sometimes it feels as though your life is a disaster. You wonder if you'll ever find joy, satisfaction, and peace. Maybe you think once you lose that ten pounds, everything will be better. Maybe you're enslaved to your work, and you think your next promotion will solve so many problems. Maybe you've been looking for fulfillment in the next drink, the next hit, the next puff, or the next conquest.

I know exactly what it's like, that unrelenting mirage of a promise that happiness is just around the next corner. Once you get there, you find a mouthful of sand instead.

If only I could get that scholarship. If only I could get married. If only my kids would obey. If only I could land that job. If only my spouse were different. If only the chemo would work.

If only.

My "if only" had partially come true when I made the Olympic team in 2008 and achieved a goal I had set as a boy. It was the American dream fulfilled. Now here I was, standing in front of thousands of Chinese fans in the first Olympics China had ever hosted. My final dive was meaningless because my previous two dives had left me far from medal contention. Nevertheless, I wanted to go out in memorable fashion. I wanted to absorb all I could of the atmosphere and the adulation. Normally I try to tune out the externals that can distract. This time, however, I looked around at the crowd. I tried to suck every bit of excitement and pleasure that I could out of my final attempt.

I enjoyed the moment. I took a deep breath and launched myself off the platform. And I turned in one of the worst dives I had ever done in a competition. The Olympics that began with such promise and potential had ended in embarrassment.

The days that followed that first Olympic experience marked a downward spiral of hopelessness and despair. My failed pursuit of Olympic glory had left me feeling abandoned and alone. I felt betrayed, rejected, and defeated by the "god" I had sacrificed everything to appease. I would have utterly scoffed at the Olympic creed declaring that the important thing "is not the triumph, but the fight; the essential thing is not to have won, but to have fought well." What nonsense that seemed to me in the aftermath of my greatest episode of heartbreak and disappointment. My whole purpose had proven hollow, and the destruction that followed left my life in tatters. I didn't know it at the time, but my purpose needed to be redirected and redeemed. *I needed to be redirected and redeemed.*

In the pages that follow, I hope to take you on a journey. Yes, it's my journey, but my goal is not simply to tell my story. My goal is to leave you with something that applies to your life. I hope you will walk away encouraged and inspired to think about your purpose in life. I hope my story helps deepen your faith. My goal is to give you hope. Because if you're struggling with self-centeredness, arrogance, and entitlement, I've been there. If you're wrestling with addiction and enslavement to pleasure, I've been there. If you're fighting against hopelessness and emptiness in life, I've been there. If you're battling fear and laziness, I've been there too. If you feel aimless, directionless, and purposeless, you're not the only one. And I can tell you absolutely and without reservation, there is hope for you.

Our hearts are made to love and to pursue meaning and purpose. Too often, though, we settle for chasing after things of inferior value—cheap imitations of the real thing. As it has for so many others, the American dream seemed to offer happiness and fulfillment but crushed me in the end when it didn't deliver. I hope through this book that you'll be provoked to think about things in a way you've never considered, and that you'll gain a new resolve on your own dreams.

I'm thankful that my story doesn't end with the failure and heartache I found in Beijing and in the days that followed. In the years since, my purpose in life has shifted and I have discovered something greater than worldly recognition and fame. Something greater than the American dream. Something far greater than even the gold medal that would ultimately be mine.

CHAPTER 1

BUILDING IDOLS

My first day in gymnastics, I peed all over the floor. That's what I remember most about my initial exposure to organized gymnastics in Lubbock, Texas.

We moved to Lubbock early in my childhood. My parents were both in the US Air Force and were stationed in Abilene when I was born in 1989. Shotgun marriages often don't last, but by the grace of God, my parents made their marriage work. My sisters Shaila and Shauni were already on the scene when I came along into what was a remarkably stable and happy family. This was not a home where Dad did his thing, Mom did her thing, and the kids did whatever they wanted. We were active—together—as a family.

That togetherness included going to church. I grew up

as a Roman Catholic, and I remember attending church regularly, Sunday after Sunday. The priest once jokingly predicted to my mom that I would grow up to become a priest—because I fell asleep in the pew almost every week. Church wasn't really important to me as a kid, but that's what we did as a family.

The move to Lubbock when I was three allowed my father to finish engineering school. Mom was still active in the air force while we were in Lubbock, but she spent most of her time taking care of my sisters and me.

I was incredibly active as a kid, running up and down the couches, jumping off things, teaching myself how to do cartwheels, and generally bouncing off the walls. One time, I tried to use the couch as a trampoline. A Diet Coke can was sitting on an end table, and as I flipped off the couch, I landed on the soda can with my lip. That was my first taste of the hospital and stitches. It wouldn't be my last. Another time, when I was about two, I decided to try to climb up the TV and came tumbling down, with the TV landing on top of me. I'm thankful that the only thing I suffered from that incident was a sprained ankle.

At four years old I finally found an outlet for my energy when I started playing soccer on an organized team (I use the word *organized* loosely—it was more like organized chaos). I had taken a lot of falls in my short life, so, understandably, I think my parents were afraid I might hurt myself even worse. So they figured they might as well make sure that I was instructed properly. That's why they added gymnastics to go along with soccer.

I remember wearing a pair of little red shorts that first day. I was scared and nervous and didn't want to tell anyone that I had to go to the bathroom. So out it came, all over the floor. Thankfully, things improved from there. It so happened that I was athletically gifted as a child. By age five, I was able to do five back handsprings in a row. I don't think that was very common, and I remember other instructors pointing me out and telling others what I could do.

From my earliest years, sports were important to me both because I enjoyed competing and because I had a special ability to perform well. I had difficulty sitting still, and I can see that trait now in my daughter. One time, when she was going crazy in her high chair, my mother-in-law remarked that Sonnie, my wife, never did that when she was a baby. My mom, however, said she was all too familiar with that behavior. My dad describes me as an "enthusiastic" child whose motor was always running.

Gymnastics would remain a large part of my life for the next several years, even after we moved to a different location. After my dad graduated from Texas Tech University, he got a job in Kokomo, Indiana, as an electrical engineer. We moved to nearby Noblesville, Indiana, when I was seven years old and would remain there until I left home for college. When I think of home, I think of Noblesville.

A northern suburb of Indianapolis, Noblesville is a fairly affluent community. It's probably a lot like what most people picture when they think of suburban life. We lived in a neighborhood with lots of houses and lots of kids. We enjoyed a fairly tight community with the families we knew from our sports activities.

Some of my best friends lived across the street from us. I remember going over to their house with my dad to build my pinewood derby car for Boy Scouts. My approach to the pinewood derby was no different than my attitude toward other sports: I wanted to win. I was super competitive as a kid, and if I didn't win, I was a terrible sport. I'd throw a fit or run off crying. When I did win, I was on top of the world. Even as a child, I craved that feeling. I loved competition and wanted to be better than everyone else, especially my sister Shauni.

Shauni is only eighteen months older than I am, and she was an extremely gifted athlete as well. We've always been close friends, and we got into some trouble and did typical kid stuff together. I remember us doing things like finding a mask and a snorkel and filling up a trash can with water. We then took turns dunking each other into the trash can, learning how to use our new equipment. When we lived in an apartment for a few years, I remember the two of us going to the Dumpster to see what kind of trash we could use to build a fort.

She was my main competition for most things throughout my childhood. If I didn't beat her, then I'd end up in a wrestling match with her. We played basketball on a hoop across the street, and Shauni says we never actually finished a game because we'd always get into a fight. I threw a basketball at her one time as she walked away. She most likely returned the favor.

We made a game out of anything we could and were cutthroat in our soccer and Go Fish competitions. We went sledding on a frozen lake when I was in second or third grade. I fell into the lake, and Shauni quickly jumped in to save the sled—not me. I'm glad she loves me more than that now. Another time, we got into a scissor fight (don't ask me to explain), and I cut her finger badly enough that she had to go to the hospital to get stitches. I swear it was an accident. I'm not sure to this day that she believes me.

I had another taste of stiches myself when I was five or six, at a roller-rink birthday party. During the limbo contest, I wanted to be the one to go the lowest and beat everyone else. But I cracked my chin open when I fell forward onto the floor while trying to go under the bar. Competitive fire was a constant motivator during my younger years, and while it got me in trouble at times, it also fueled my quest for excellence.

Despite all our shenanigans, we had a remarkably

structured childhood. I guess that comes naturally from having two military parents. We ate dinner together in the evenings. When we disobeyed, my parents put us in time-out. We were expected to do chores when we were told, and my mom often used the competitiveness between Shauni and me to her advantage, getting us to do the tasks that we didn't like to do. "Okay," she'd say, "let's see who can take the trash out the quickest."

A lot of my friends came from homes with far fewer guidelines. But before I could go play, I had to cut the grass or do other tasks that needed to be done. My parents had high expectations for us. I hated the restrictions at the time, but I have since come to see the wisdom and the benefit of them. My parents put guidelines in place not because they didn't like us but because they wanted what was best for us—what would keep us safe and balanced as individuals later in life.

My parents remained active in the Catholic church after we moved to Noblesville. Both my mom and my dad taught Sunday school, so the church community stayed a big part of my life. While I had a church background complete with things like Vacation Bible School and Sunday school, the teaching didn't seem to apply to the rest of my life away from the church.

Eventually, sports began to push church more and

more to the periphery of my life. Sports were becoming what I lived for. Sports captured my dreams, hopes, and imagination, and thus my allegiance. I looked to sports to give my life meaning and happiness. Isn't that what we are all looking for—meaning and happiness? For me, sports seemed to be the best avenue for getting what I wanted. So sports became what I would worship and where I would place my time, energy, resources, and affections.

In one sense, this was what the Bible refers to as *idolatry*. For a long time when I heard the word *idol*, I thought of some carved statue with people bowing down before it. Or maybe I thought of someone you look up to, like a pop star. But I've learned that an idol is anything we worship that isn't God, anything that captures the affections, devotions, and desires that only God deserves. If something drives us, gives us meaning, and shapes and forms how we live, and that thing isn't God, then it's an idol. It took me a long time to figure this out, but the truth is our hearts were created to worship something. It will either be God or something else.

As I said, sports became my idol. But in another sense, they were a stepping-stone. Sports were my ticket to attaining my real idols: comfort, ease, notoriety, fame, pleasure, power, and control. These controlled my heart. I believed if I could just attain these things, they would give me the satisfaction, joy, and security that I desperately sought at my core.

We like to describe our quest for such things as "pursuing the American dream." I bought in to that pursuit at an early age. "The American dream" sounds so much nobler than "I want more stuff," but that's what it comes down to, at least for me. We want our houses, we want our cars, we want our security. But what we ultimately want is fulfillment and happiness, and we think these things will provide them. We were built with a yearning for satisfaction, joy, and security, and that in itself isn't wrong. The problem comes when we look for these things in the wrong places.

That's why sports became such an obsession for me. They were my tool to attain what I loved. And what I loved, more than anything else, was health, wealth, and prosperity for myself. That's what drove me, and so I threw myself ever more fully into sports.

CHAPTER 2

AN OLYMPIC DREAM

I watched my first Olympics in 1996, when I was seven years old. My mom loved to watch the Olympics, and since I was competing in gymnastics at the time, I was especially interested in watching with her. In fact, the Olympics were a big deal for the whole family. Rather than watching TV shows or movies in the evening, when the Olympics came around, we gathered around the TV together to watch the games.

I can still picture the images of those Atlanta Olympics like they were yesterday. Amy Chow slipped off the balance beam and smacked her face in the process. Dominique Moceanu fell on two vaults. Kerri Strug did the same on her first vault attempt. But then, something magical happened. Strug had suffered a painful ankle injury on her first vault, hobbling off the mat. As she lined up for her second attempt, she looked at her coach, Bela Karolyi, for much-needed encouragement.

"You can do it," Karolyi told her. "You can do it. You can do it."

And Strug did, nailing her final vault to give the US women the gold medal—the first ever for the United States in the women's team competition. I'll never forget the image of Karolyi carrying Strug up to the podium and the look of joy on their faces. Because of my own involvement in gymnastics, watching the Magnificent Seven win that medal stoked my competitive fires. Competing in the Olympics became my focus, my inspiration, my dream, my god. I was going to be an Olympian. Not only that, but I was going to win—and I would revel in the fame and the celebrity it brought. And in the years that followed, I bowed at the feet of gods fashioned of gold, silver, and bronze.

From that point forward, I always perked up when I heard the Olympic theme song playing. My birthday and Christmas presents were always Olympic themed. One Christmas I received a pair of white shoes with the Olympic rings on them. They weren't cool, but I loved them.

Though I played baseball occasionally, I spent more time playing soccer. I could run really fast and was often able to take control of the field. You win in soccer by scoring the most goals, so I always wanted to be the one to score all those goals—not necessarily for the benefit of the team, but to get the glory for myself. So I could be exalted, to use an old-fashioned word.

Now, I'll stop right here because you may be thinking that sounds a little arrogant. And it was. But guess what? I'm not alone in this. If we're honest, we all crave the praise and acceptance of other people. Maybe you compare what she's wearing to your outfit. Maybe you compare his income to yours. You see? That's a desire to be exalted as well. We want to be valued and loved, and we want others to think highly of us.

Here's how it worked for me. If we lost 5–4, but I scored all four of our goals, I might be frustrated by the loss, but part of me would be happy because of how well I did. And I certainly wouldn't take any responsibility for losing. My heart would scream, *"Hello, look at me! I scored all four goals!"* Even now, this remains a struggle for me. I'm constantly tempted to blame others for my failures rather than accepting responsibility for myself. That's the typical human response to mistakes and screw-ups: we shift blame, we minimize, we deflect, we excuse, we hide, we justify. It's been this way since the beginning of time. We've always had trouble accepting and acknowledging that we've done something wrong. Adam blamed Eve. Eve blamed the serpent. And so began the trend that has persisted through human history.

When I started getting into the more advanced travel leagues, the ones that traveled longer distances to compete against other travel teams, I failed to make the A team my first year. I hated that. It bugged me to no end that I wasn't the best and was relegated instead to the B team. That only made me work harder, until I eventually played my way onto the A team. Once I got there, I never lost that spot.

Soccer was fun, but gymnastics was where I excelled, and I knew that was my ticket to the Olympics—my tool for attaining ultimate happiness and satisfaction. I'd sometimes spend five hours a day doing gymnastics, especially during the summer. My mom took a job at the gym to help pay for my lessons. We were there constantly. During the school year, I'd head to the facility for practice immediately after school and would stay until late in the evening while my mom finished up her work.

That makes it sound like I worked hard, and I often did. But I was lazy as well, often choosing to live by my feelings rather than what I should have done. If I could find a loophole to get out of the work, I'd take it. I fight against that attitude even today. I might schedule a workout, but I'll tell myself that it isn't as necessary as my coach thinks it is. So I'll slack off.

I don't think that sense of laziness is exclusive to me.

It's human nature, and it's rampant in sports, believe it or not. When people say they give 110 percent, I'm not convinced they're being honest. As athletes, we too often look for ways to cut corners in our quest to excel. There's always something more we could do in our training: more mental training, eating better, sleeping more or less. But the important principle is to not live based on how we feel. Whether in athletics or any other area of life, either we can choose what is easy now and guarantee more difficult circumstances later, or we can choose to pursue the difficult now and reap the rewards later.

We started a boys' team at a gymnastics facility in Noblesville. Another boy and I quickly went through four different coaches because we were so difficult to work with. We were rebellious and didn't respect their authority. We were stubborn. We would refuse to do things our coaches told us to do if we thought they were dumb. Sounds like a dream coaching job, no?

I was proud. I was arrogant. I was self-centered. I wasn't interested in gymnastics for a legitimate reason like wanting to get the most out of the abilities God had given me. I was interested in gymnastics because I saw it as the path for my own glorification, for the accolades and praise of others. Even the Olympics, as much as I wanted to achieve that, didn't provide compelling enough motivation for me to work hard. That was too far off in the future.

My immediate motivation was the desire to win the next competition. Or sometimes it was something more short-term. If I were especially grumpy, my mom or my coach would offer me a piece of candy if I'd do four circles on "the mushroom." The mushroom is an apparatus similar to the pommel horse, which is one of the events you'll see in beginning levels of gymnastics competitions. Gymnasts use it to learn to pivot around on their hands. The mushroom is a stepping-stone to the pommel horse. I absolutely hated the mushroom, but I'd do the work for that immediate gratification of the candy.

Still, even though I didn't work like I should have, and even though I was rebellious and difficult to work with, I succeeded in gymnastics. I didn't often lose in my competitions. In my very first meet as a competitive gymnast, sometime in third grade, I scored a 9 out of 10. I didn't know what that meant at the time, but I knew I'd won the event, and that was all that mattered. My sister had a basketball game after that competition, and I proudly wore my medal around my neck the whole time I was at her game. I often took all the ribbons I won at competitions and lined them up in a nice, neat row in front of me and posed for photographs behind them. My bedroom was decorated with my medals and ribbons hanging from rods that my dad installed on the walls.

During competition season, we traveled all over the state. Every once in a while we would travel outside the state for bigger competitions, but that was rare. Winning state was my biggest accomplishment in gymnastics, and that felt awesome. I thought I was hot stuff. My parents praised me. My coaches praised me. Winning fed my desire for recognition and acceptance.

I didn't discover until later just how enslaving that type of mind-set is. When you live for the praise of other people, you can never be satisfied. The ecstasy from a win today quickly fades, and you have to win tomorrow to recapture that high. It's a relentless, unsatisfying, and elusive quest when you are fueled by the pursuit of your own glory.

It's also exhausting. No matter how much praise you get, it doesn't completely satisfy you. You'll always go back for more. I was on that treadmill for years until I found freedom (which we'll talk about later).

Amid all my striving, however, I did learn and develop some positive traits, despite my flaws. Persistence was one. I was a persistent kid. For instance, when traveling around the state for gymnastics competitions, I would see water towers in different towns with the town name prominently painted on them. My town, Noblesville, had a water tower, but it didn't have "Noblesville" written on it. I thought it should.

So I began a letter-writing campaign to the mayor, lobbying for the addition of "Noblesville" to our water tower.

If I didn't get a response or see any progress toward that end, I would write again. And again. Eventually, the city name got added to the tower. I still don't have any idea if it was because of my efforts or something else entirely, but I like to think persistence paid off in that case!

Despite my success in gymnastics, I eventually got burned out on the sport. I began dreading practice when I was about eleven years old. The sport had occupied so much of my time for so many years, with practice four or five times a week, that it seemed like gymnastics was all I was ever doing. It didn't leave me time to play with my friends or get involved with anything else. I didn't stop the sport suddenly, but I slowly transitioned and took lessons less and less often. Part of this had to do with being tired of gymnastics, and part of it had to do with something else.

I had discovered diving.

CHAPTER 3

TAKING A DIVE

In fall 2000, I had a good friend whose family won diving lessons in an auction. She was the same age as I was, and her sister played soccer with my sister. Our families were close. They invited me to come along for the diving lessons.

Water was already a big part of my life. Though I never competed in swimming, I took swimming lessons, and our family swam a lot for fun. We went regularly to a lake near our home to go boating. I loved the water, but diving just hadn't been on my radar.

My first lesson was on a 1-meter springboard with a coach who wore yellow sunglasses. He took me through a couple of different techniques and taught me a forward one-and-a-half flip for the first time.

Hey, this isn't that bad, I thought. I discovered that diving was quite similar to gymnastics. I got to flip through the air, which was fun. I got to be acrobatic. In essence, diving was gymnastics over water, with the main difference being that I was now landing on my head instead of on my feet. I loved the thrill that came with the free fall and the adrenaline that surged through my body when I flipped through the air.

I also liked the team aspect. In gymnastics, there was only one other boy on my team, so I was a bit lonely. Diving gave me an opportunity to compete with more team members.

Here's what I didn't love: the terrible suits divers have to wear. My first day of diving I cringed at the thought of wearing briefs like that. Everyone makes fun of the "Speedo guy" at the beach, and rightfully so. Likewise, my friends and I used to make fun of divers and their itty-bitty briefs. So let's just get that out of the way right now. The suits are awful, even if they do help with mobility in flipping and twisting. Swimming trunks are too restrictive for such movements, so divers have no choice but to wear briefs. But it doesn't make them any less terrible.

The required apparel notwithstanding, I went back again to the lessons. And again. I began to see improvement in the pool, and I fed off that sense of progression. I continued with my lessons, and I eventually began to compete. I don't remember much about my first diving competition or how I actually fared, except that it took place at the high school in the town next to ours. They required us to fill out a sheet with the list of dives we were going to do in the competition. I had to learn a whole new set of lingo.

For example, all dives fall into one of six categories:

1. **Front,** which is your basic, forward-facing dive
2. **Back,** where you stand backward on the board or platform and flip backward into the pool
3. **Reverse/gainer** (the terms are interchangeable), where you face forward on the board and flip backward after takeoff
4. **Inward,** where you stand backward and flip forward upon takeoff
5. **Twist,** where you rotate yourself in a corkscrew-like turn
6. **Armstand,** where you start off in a handstand

Reverse and inward dives are the most dangerous ones because you're spinning back toward the board. Typically, if a diver hits the board or the platform, it's during a dive from one of those two categories. When Greg Louganis hit his head on the board in the 1988 Olympics in Seoul, that was a reverse/gainer. He began the dive facing forward and flipped backward, but he didn't get far enough away from the board on his launch.

Within each category, another number designates how many half somersaults or half twists you do. A front one-and-a-half would be 103 (1 for front and 3 for the number of half flips). A front double would be 104.

But it gets more complex than that. At the end of each dive number is the position in which you are doing the dive. *A* is for straight, *B* is for pike, *C* is for tuck, and *D* is for free. A tuck is when you fold your knees into your shoulders, making a ball with your body. A pike is when you bring your legs straight toward your face. Your knees are by your face, but your legs are completely straight.

In Olympic diving, you rarely see an *A*. So a front dive pike would be 101B. If the announcer says a diver is doing a 101C, that's a front dive in the tuck position. A back armstand, which is only done on platform, double two-and-a-half twist would be 6245 (6 for armstand, 2 for backward, 4 for the number of half flips, and 5 for the number of half twists). Yes, it's difficult to understand sometimes, but that shows the complexity of the sport.

For divers, coaches, officials, judges, commentators, and anybody else involved in a meet, looking at the combination of numbers and letters will let them know exactly what a diver is doing. In Olympic competition, men perform six dives while women do five dives. There's also a formula that measures how hard a dive is: that's your degree of difficulty, or DD. A complex and elaborate formula determines how difficult a dive is based on all the dive's components.

In scoring, judges typically look at three things:

takeoff, midair position, and entry into the water. A diver's takeoff needs to be the correct distance from the board or platform—not too close, not too far away. The midair position should be clean and tight. For example, in the pike position, the knees can't be bent. Toes must always be pointed, and divers have to look like they're in control of the dive.

The entry is the most important part as far as judging goes; judges often weigh more of their scores on the entry. A clean entry with no splash at all will usually result in a higher score than a dive with an amazing takeoff and gorgeous midair position but a heavier entry.

If you finish a dive high and have a clean entry, judges love that. It shows you have power from your takeoff that translates into the air and that you control your lineup into the water. Position going into the water must be vertical. It's better to be "short" on a dive (meaning you haven't gotten to the vertical point yet) rather than "over," (meaning you've gone past the vertical point).

Scores range from 0 to 10 in half-point increments. Dives that score 10 are considered to be excellent dives, while 8.5–9.5 are very good, 7–8 are good, 5–6.5 are satisfactory, 2.5–4.5 are deficient, .5–2 are unsatisfactory, and 0 is a completely failed dive. Multiple judges score a dive and provide the raw score. The raw score is the total after a certain number of judges' marks are thrown out (this number varies based on the competition level). To give the final score for the dive, the raw score is then multiplied by the degree of difficulty.

If all that sounds like gibberish to you, that's understandable. It was gibberish to me, too, when I started.

I wasn't an outstanding diver at first. By no means was I any kind of prodigy. Thomas Finchum, who would later be my Olympic synchronized diving partner, was the one who was the prodigy. We practiced together regularly, and I was always in Thomas's shadow, but he was encouraging to me and was quick to tell people how good I was going to be.

I didn't make nationals the winter after I started diving competitively, even though the rest of my teammates did. The following summer, however, I advanced to nationals for the first time. My drive to win was powerful. It's why I kept working at it even when I wasn't succeeding. I knew my gymnastics background gave me a strong base to build on, and I knew I should have been able to excel in diving. So I kept at it.

As a teenager, I'd spend hours each day working to improve. In addition to the work I did in the pool at the Indiana University Natatorium in downtown Indianapolis, practice consisted of heavy conditioning work such as cardio, circuit training, and weight training. But the closest thing to diving on land was the belt and harness system that was usually suspended over a trampoline or over mats. Once

I attached the belt and harness and hooked up the ropes, the coach would pull me through each dive using a pulley system. That setup allowed me to practice and hone the movements and the mechanics that are necessary to execute each dive. If I was nervous about a dive, the belt and harness gave me more of a feel for it and let me repeat it over and over. Working on dry ground let me get more repetitions than I would get in the pool. The nice thing about it was the safety system: I didn't fall flat on my face if I messed up.

The bad part about it was how tedious it was. I'd have to repeat the same jumps, the same small movements again and again. I always wanted to do the bigger dives, and I hated having to work on the details so much. Yet years later, I can still hear my coach repeating, "Details make champions."

As for conditioning, flexibility and core work were the keys. Flexibility wasn't a strength of mine in the early years of diving, but I knew I'd have to pursue it if I wanted to be a better diver. So I'd lie in bed at night doing the side splits, often falling asleep in that position.

My parents made significant sacrifices to help me pursue my dreams. Lessons for both gymnastics and diving are expensive, and that's why my mom began working for my gymnastics coach and the club's management—so I could train for free. But my sisters were involved with sports as well, and those didn't come with discounts. Money was tight.

My mom sacrificed a lot of her time for me. Once I started diving, I was practicing five or six days a week in Indianapolis at a pool about an hour away from home. Mom set up carpools with another diver so they could share the transportation time and expense. She would drive us to practice, and the other mom would drive us home. That was still a two-hour commitment from her each day, just to drive me to practice.

Sometimes, though, the carpool wouldn't work out for one reason or another. On those days, she'd pick me up at school at two in the afternoon, drive an hour to practice, stay there with me for about four hours, and then drive an hour home. That was six hours of her day that she wasn't spending at home with my sisters or my dad. Mom really had to give up a lot of her time for me to train, and I can't tell you how grateful I am for her efforts.

My sisters like to joke now that our childhood was all about me. The basement of our house was almost a shrine to my achievements and accolades. They tease, "Oh, this entire big wall here is dedicated to David's accomplishments. But look, here's Shauni's little corner, and here's Shaila's little corner." I'm sure they must have felt some animosity earlier in our childhood, but they never expressed it or joked with me about it until we grew closer after we grew up. They, too, had to make sacrifices for me, and I am thankful for their graciousness.

Our family life almost always revolved around sporting

events. Shaila stopped playing sports when she went to high school, but Shauni was sold out to soccer. She was good enough to play collegiately for an NCAA Division I school, so she was traveling almost nonstop with her high school team. She often got rides to games and practices with teammates because Mom was busy transporting me to practice. We occasionally had schedule conflicts between my schedule and Shauni's, but we accommodated them the best we could.

When I was younger, my family had dinner together almost every night. But the older I got, the more family meals decreased in frequency. Diving practice consumed almost all my high school years, making it necessary for me to eat on the road or whenever I could grab a bite. I spent lots of time with my mom driving back and forth to practice, but our family time as a whole took a major hit once I began diving more.

The more I improved, the more devoted I became to diving. My dry-ground-training facility on the west side of Indianapolis was located at an old mental hospital about ten minutes away from the IU Natatorium where I did my water practices. Back in the 1950s, the state lost funding for the hospital and shut it down. My coach acquired this spot for our training in the basement of one of the buildings on the hospital campus.

The previous tenants had pretty much walked away leaving everything intact, so every time I walked down to the basement I'd go past desks and overturned filing cabinets. The basement was home to a huge, open gym that we turned into our own space by bringing in mats, trampolines, diving boards, exercise equipment, harnesses, and everything we needed in order to train.

Upstairs on the main level was more of a classroom setting. One of the rooms up there had a huge diving library with videos from every major competition—the Olympics, the world cup, the world championships, and on and on. I checked out videos constantly and watched them repeatedly, analyzing and dissecting the technique of the world's greatest divers and trying to figure out what made them so good.

Still, as committed as I was to improving, training wasn't always easy. At times it was downright petrifying— especially when I had to attempt the 10-meter platform. I'd been diving for a couple of years when the time came to make this progression. In the Olympics, the diving events are the 3-meter springboard and the 10-meter platform. Typically the older divers excel at the 3-meter because they're bigger and stronger and can push the board down more, thus propelling them higher on their dives. The younger divers are usually the best at the 10-meter platform. So my coach thought it was time for me to begin learning it. And I wanted to learn it. Well, sometimes . . .

The fact is, ten meters is the equivalent of a three-story building. Jumping from that high into a pool would be terrifying for just about anyone, even if you've spent years preparing for it. And I had. My diving lessons moved me incrementally higher toward the 10-meter goal, so it's not as if I were going straight from 1 meter to 10. I had mastered 7.5 meters without too much trouble.

But the 10-meter was another issue altogether. That was the highest platform in the building. I knew I could get hurt from that high. The immediate risk is on the takeoff, when you have to make sure that you clear the platform. You have to jump far enough out that you don't hit your arm, your leg, or your head, because that can cause serious injury. In 1983, Soviet diver Sergei Chalibashvili died after hitting his head on the platform while attempting a three-and-a-half reverse somersault tuck. I'm thankful I've never experienced anything like that. I've never torn my shoulder or broken any bones. I have, however, hit the platform a couple of times with my fingers and toes, which breaks the skin and causes abrasions.

Another risk is the water itself. At that height, the water is not anything close to soft. Hitting the water from ten meters is like hitting a ton of bricks. When I was first learning to dive from ten meters, I smacked the water a lot—a back smack, a belly smack, a leg smack, and so forth. *Smacking* is what happens when you don't enter the water cleanly. It absolutely annihilates you when you do that, and it makes you not want to climb up that platform ever again. The pain is intense.

I often woke up in the morning with bruises from smacking the day before. It was kind of a joke around the pool that the next day we wanted to see each other's bruises from our smacks. I've seen divers whose backs have bled from smacking the water. Sometimes you can even see the imprint of a ripple of water on a diver's leg or back after they smack.

By the time I started diving from ten meters, I'd seen other divers get hurt from that height, and I'd experienced the pain myself from failed dives at lower heights. Plus, I knew if I didn't execute a dive properly and smacked the water, I'd be embarrassed in front of everybody. I developed a healthy fear and respect for that height that I still have today.

I'd learn the dives in practice outside the pool, but when it came time to perform them from the platform, I wouldn't do them. I'd dillydally in the stairwell, killing time until practice was over. Or, at worst, I'd bawl my eyes out because I was so scared. Crying was my last resort to get out of the dive. I was usually pretty guarded about other people seeing me cry, so I didn't shed tears that often. That should tell you how petrified I was. Sometimes on the way to practice I'd make excuses to my mom as to why I couldn't go that day: "I don't feel well" or "I'm too tired."

This went on for a while, until my mom started offering incentives. She offered me a CD if I'd just do the dive I had been practicing. After much cajoling and encouraging from my mom and my coach, John Wingfield, I eventually took the plunge. I don't remember much about that very first dive from ten meters, but my fear of the platform continued to plague me for years. Eventually a sports psychologist helped me conquer most of my fear and taught me how to be more structured in my mental approach. The mental aspect to diving is the most important part of the sport. If you're not able to master your emotions and control your thinking, you won't be a successful diver. The physical component is obviously crucial, but the mental component separates the good divers from the great ones.

In fact, my work with a sports psychologist was pivotal for my career. The insights I gained from him were invaluable. With his help, I learned to set goals—both goals for the training process and goals for the outcome. Ultimately, my goal was to get to the Olympics. That was my outcome goal. Once I had identified that outcome goal, I set it aside and focused instead on the process goals—the little goals along the way designed to help me get to the outcome goal. The principle is that the more detailed the goals, the more achievable they become, and the more one accomplishes in return. Remember what my coach always said? "Details make champions."

When it came to the 10-meter platform, one of my process goals was to conquer that fear and take another step toward my goal of the Olympics. Now, how would I accomplish that process goal? I set more process goals.

I learned relaxation exercises and began to visualize the dives in my head. The relaxation techniques helped me learn to control my heart rate and keep my anxiety level low. One of my former gymnastics coaches also helped with the visualization component by suggesting that I draw out the motions of my 10-meter dives. So that's what I did. I took a pen and paper and drew the dives, move by move, as I saw them in my head.

My mom's incentive tactics worked only so long. As I progressed as a diver, I needed a stronger motivation to get me off that platform and into the water. I vividly remember standing on the 10-meter platform, looking down at the rest of the divers doing their work at different levels and thinking to myself, *What am I doing now that's going to get me to where I want to be? If I want to make the Olympic Games, then what am I doing right now that's going to help accomplish that?*

Walking down the stairs and refusing to take the plunge wasn't going to help me achieve my goal. I had to push through my fear and the lies I had believed. I had to push past the thought that I wasn't ready, that my coach didn't have my best interests at heart, that I would forget everything I had learned, and get off the platform. That realization was critical for my career. These techniques didn't work every time; I didn't get over my fear immediately. Gradually, though, it became easier and easier to make those dives. I wish I could say that such fear is now a thing of the past, but it's not. Especially if I haven't dived for a while, I still experience a twinge of timidity when I step onto that platform. I don't think it will ever go away completely.

There are two types of fear: healthy and unhealthy. Healthy fear prevents you from doing things that might harm yourself or others. That's good fear. But the other kind of fear, the unhealthy kind, comes from a place that it took me a long time to identify. When we worry about something that might happen, we tend to doubt God's goodness and his sovereignty, his control over everything. At its root, fear is a failure to trust in God. I often have to remind myself of that when I'm tempted to let fear take root in my heart.

I was making progress in individual competition. At the Speedo National Diving Championships (those suits again!) in 2003, I placed nineteenth on the 1-meter, twelfth on the 3-meter, and second on the 10-meter. At the same event the following year, I moved up to fourth in the 1-meter and second on the 3-meter. I dropped one place to third in the 10-meter.

In the synchronized diving competition, though, the results were even better. Synchronized diving, or "synchro," is the event where two divers compete as a team. You do almost the exact same dives as in individual competition, but right next to your teammate. The goal is for the two divers to be perfectly synchronized so they look like one diver going into the water.

Thomas Finchum was my first synchronized diving partner. We started working together in 2002, but by 2003 we were one of the most promising teams of young divers in the country. We placed seventh in the Speedo National Diving Championships in 2003 and improved on that in 2004, finishing fifth in the FINA Diving World Cup Trials and third in the Speedo American Cup.

USA Diving is the nonprofit organization that powers and organizes American competitive diving and prepares teams for competition. It periodically changes how divers can qualify for the Olympics and even the Olympic Trials, and I don't remember what the criteria were at the time. We probably had to place in the top three in the Speedo American Cup, which is a big senior-level meet, or in the top seven at a national championship. However it happened, Thomas and I qualified for the Olympic Trials in 2004, when I was fifteen.

Honestly, we were surprised that we had made it to the trials. We didn't think we were a strong enough team to be there. But we knew this was an opportunity to gain valuable experience that could help us in our efforts to qualify for the Beijing Olympics in 2008. In the 2004 trials, we had absolutely no plans or expectations that we would advance to the Olympics. Those trials were simply process goals.

On any given day in the sport of diving, you can bomb, or you can dive amazingly well and do better than anyone expects. That's what happened with Thomas and me during the trials. After the preliminaries, we were only six points away from first place, and the first-place team was going to the Olympics. Six points, by the way, is a tiny margin. It's the difference of pointing your toe harder or going in the water two degrees more vertical. It's miniscule.

We had another good day in the finals, but the team of Mark Ruiz and Kyle Prandi fared a little bit better. They widened the gap and won the competition while we finished third. We hadn't qualified for the Olympics, but I was ecstatic with the result. We had done far more than we set out to do, and we had surprised a lot of people in the process. Those 2004 Olympic Trials were a jump-start to my diving career. They transformed me from being a decent diver into being an Olympic-caliber diver. From that point forward, the 2008 Olympics weren't just a pipe dream. They were well within my grasp, and I knew it.

The sad part about it was that even if we had won the competition, I probably would have been disqualified shortly thereafter. The Olympic drug testing would have been my undoing.

CHAPTER 4

THE FOOL
AND HIS FOLLY

I began experimenting with marijuana just before my eighth-grade year. My oldest sister had started the habit when she was a freshman in high school, so I had been around it since sixth grade. When I hung out with her and her friends, I witnessed the suburban drug culture—the camaraderie that came with doing drugs together and the peer pressure to do it because everyone else was. Sometimes I'd even help her get the marijuana ready to smoke.

A couple of years later, I was ready to try it myself. I had been goofing around with three or four of my friends for a while, and we were an ornery bunch. We'd throw snowballs at cars. We'd ring doorbells and run away. We'd toilet paper houses. Eventually, such shenanigans stopped satisfying us, and we longed for more.

My friends started using marijuana before I did. After a while I decided I wanted to be like my friends and do what they were doing. I wanted to experience it for myself. For one thing, it was a thrill. I enjoyed the risk of getting caught. I also enjoyed the high that came with smoking.

Cigarette smoking began about the same time as the marijuana. I was keenly influenced by peer pressure and was desperate to fit in with my friends. Since I was so heavily involved in diving, I wasn't able to spend a lot of time with them, and I wanted to be accepted. Smoking marijuana and cigarettes was a way for me to feel like I was a "normal kid."

But the rationale and the desire went deeper. At that point, my sole purpose in life was essentially to do whatever gave me pleasure. I had no spiritual mentors and no depth of thought or instruction about what my life's purpose truly was. So I bought in to the lie that immediate gratification was the highest priority. At that time, being accepted by my friends satisfied me the most, so I went along with what I thought would gain their approval. I was living only for the next best thing that would fulfill me the quickest. It was a mentality that enslaved me for years. Maybe you know what I'm talking about.

Substance abuse might not be your weakness, but if

you're honest, you'll admit that you look for immediate gratification elsewhere. Perhaps it's a shopping binge that you think will meet your needs. Maybe it's a new truck. Or a new boyfriend or girlfriend. Or overindulging in food. Or attaining the perfect body. Whatever the specifics, we all have a need to fill the emptiness in our lives. My problem was that I was looking in the wrong places to fill that void.

My rebellion morphed again in high school when I started drinking regularly to go along with the marijuana and cigarettes. Since we weren't old enough to buy booze, my friends and I would go garage hopping. In suburban neighborhoods it's often common for people to leave their garage doors open all the time, even at night. My friends and I would go through neighborhoods looking for open garage doors, then we'd check to see if the garage had a refrigerator in it. Those fridges would often be full of alcohol, which we would pilfer to supply our habit.

I never thought that my use of drugs or alcohol was especially problematic when I was a teenager. For the most part, these habits didn't control my life, and they rarely played a role in my diving. One exception to that was at the 2004 Olympic Trials, when I made the foolish decision to smoke marijuana a few days before. I would have failed a drug test had I ended up making the Olympic team that year. After that, I drank on the weekends, but my marijuana use was much less frequent. In fact, years later in 2008, I pledged not to drink alcohol at all because I thought abstaining would help me as a diver.

Cigarettes, however, were another story. I used them as a tool to help cope with the pressures of competitive diving. Gradually, cigarettes came to have a death grip on my life. It started with maybe one cigarette a day, then two or three. Then I needed to have one before practice and after practice. Smoking is rampant in the diving community, both in the United States and in other countries. Since diving is not a cardiovascular sport that requires a great lung capacity, divers think that smoking doesn't affect their performance.

For me, one of the allures of smoking was control. Since I was so desperate to control my life and the circumstances surrounding me, I saw smoking as something I could control. If I was nervous or anxious before a competition, I could run out and smoke a cigarette to help me gain composure. I could control the cigarette in my hand. I could use it until it was out. I was able to be God in that moment, and that's what my heart's greatest desire was—to be God. When you don't have an eternal God to whom you are submitting, you quickly turn to lesser gods to fill that hole. Cigarettes were the means to get the control I craved for my life.

I was terribly deceived about a lot of things, including my cigarette use. I thought it was a way for me to exercise control, but really the opposite was true—the cigarettes were controlling me. I had to have them. Even when I became a Christian several years later, I continued to struggle with my desire for cigarettes. I'd smoke and try to hide it from my wife, who hated the habit. She'd sometimes find a pack of cigarettes in my bag, and my cover would be blown. Even today, if I let my guard down, I could easily fall back into it. I could start believing that smoking promises me freedom and will make me happy. In reality, it would make me its slave and control my life.

The 2004 Olympic Trials gave me a taste of the success I might have in making my Olympic dream come true. I absolutely loved it. My surprising performance in those trials provided some much-needed motivation. Though I continued to wrestle with the fear of diving from ten meters, my desire for the Olympics outweighed that fear. I began to learn more individual dives so I could improve my 10-meter performance and not be limited to synchro.

I advanced to the national championships a couple of months later and reveled in the recognition and fame that was starting to come my way. In October 2004, I made my first international trip to compete in my first junior world championships in Brazil. My performance there was abysmal, and I finished near the bottom. Not to be defeated, I made my first senior international meet in 2005 in

Moscow, then qualified for the big-time later that year—
the World Aquatics Championships in Montreal. This was
the best of the best. No longer limited by age groups, the
competition was open to anyone who was good enough to
be there. I struggled again, finishing in twenty-sixth place.

But these events were just stepping-stones for me.
Although I hadn't tasted a lot of success at this point, making it to the world stage was rewarding and made me want
to work even harder. Even the poor performances helped
me discover gaps in my training and deficiencies that I
could address and improve upon.

Encouraging signs abounded. After the 2004 Olympics,
most of the top US men's divers retired from the sport. I was
in the next cadre of up-and-coming divers behind them.
With such strong competition out of the way, my path to
success had cleared considerably.

Thomas Finchum was not just my synchro partner, he
was also my main competition. Since we had grown up
together and been diving with each other since 2002, we
were like brothers—in every sense of the word. We would
bicker like brothers and we would be friends like brothers
when we worked as a team.

At the same time, we were competing against each other
individually, but it was still awesome. We pushed each other
to excel. Yes, we were competitors, but we were also good

friends. Because I trained with him, my game improved. He motivated me and stretched me. I owe Thomas a great deal and would not be the diver I am today without him.

After our surprising display at the 2004 Olympic Trials, Thomas and I improved quickly, and we started to dominate the sport. He was better in 2005, while I had the edge in 2006. He was back on top in 2007, while I regained the advantage in 2008. And so it went.

We placed first in synchro at the Speedo National Diving Championships in 2005. We did it again in the Speedo US Open and the Kaiser Permanente National Diving Championships in 2006. We won first place in the Speedo USA Diving Spring National Championships and the Kaiser Permanente National Diving Championships in 2007. We won gold in the Pan American Games and the AT&T USA Diving Grand Prix in 2007. We were on fire, and I experienced similar gains in individual competition. I won first in the Speedo US Open and the Kaiser Permanente National Championships in 2006.

That success fueled our fire and raised our confidence even more. And it made me jubilant that I was becoming somebody in the diving world. I was quick to google myself to see what others were saying about me. Sometimes friends would pass along articles to my parents, and I always wanted to read them. I was obsessed with how I was perceived. I wanted writers to recognize me when I excelled, and I wanted them to gloss over the times I performed poorly. All the attention fed my pride. It stroked my ego. I figured it was only a matter of time before lasting fame and happiness were mine.

While I enjoyed what Thomas and I were achieving as a team, I wanted more than anything to be just as successful in individual competition. I wanted to be the only one in the spotlight, and I wanted Thomas to play in the background. Yes, it was great when we medaled in synchro; we could experience that fame together, but ultimately, my pride made me crave the limelight for myself. And I was beginning to accomplish it in 2008.

My first individual medal in international competition came in 2008 at the FINA Diving World Cup in Beijing. I finished third. For the first time, I felt like I had learned how to compete. I learned how to match my mental game with my physical game, and I had the bronze medal to show for it. At the international level, the goal for any competition is simply to be on the podium. Winning first, second, or third isn't necessarily that different (unless you're China, and gold is the only objective). That's because of the fickle nature of the sport; so many different divers can win on any given day. In a lot of sports, second or third place may feel like a failure, but for us it is a major achievement. I had achieved it in that Olympic warm-up event in 2004, and I figured that I could replicate that success in the Beijing Olympics in 2008.

USA Diving was struggling at that time. The US team

had been a dominant player on the international scene for years. Greg Louganis is the most famous diver in US history, winning silver in the 1976 Olympics and gold in 1984 and 1988, but many others had contributed to the US's success. In 1984, for example, US athletes won eight diving medals. That number dropped to five medals in 1988, then to three in 1992, two in 1996, and one in 2000. Then the US team failed to medal in the 2004 Olympics in Athens. It was another disappointing performance for USA Diving.

Before the 2008 Olympics in Beijing, then, the pressure on the US diving team was immense. Another failure like Athens could mean a loss of funding. USA Diving isn't a large organization, so sponsorships are a huge part of its success. And sponsorships are tough to come by for an organization that isn't producing winners.

Because Thomas and I had been performing so well for so long leading up to the Olympic Trials, we didn't really have to worry about whether we would make the Olympic team in 2008. We were shoo-ins, both individually and as a synchro team. Our spot on the Olympic team wasn't going to be based solely on how we competed in the trials. The selection committee for USA Diving was determined to field the best team possible, regardless of the outcome of one event.

Still, I left no room for doubt and won first place in the US Olympic Team Trials in 2008 in individual competition. The dream I had pursued so relentlessly for so long was finally becoming a reality. I was heading to the Olympics.

The realization of that achievement hit me in waves. One wave came when I actually won the competition in front of so many fans. Another came when one of my former teammates passed on his Olympic ring to me—a ring provided by USA Diving with the Olympic symbol on it—so I could wear it until my own ring was ready. That's a tradition among divers, and wearing his ring was a huge deal for me.

In Indianapolis, you also get your name written on the wall at the IU Natatorium. It's a tradition, whether you are a diver or a swimmer. When I was growing up, I had studied the names on that wall—the many outstanding athletes who had qualified for the Olympics at that pool. The wall was a constant and visible reminder to me of what I was striving for. Now my own name would join the ranks of those whose names I had been reading for years.

Qualifying for the Olympics made me think I was really something special. My pride swelled even more, and my ego climbed to gargantuan levels. During the last day of competition at the Olympic Trials in Indianapolis, I left the pool and went to run some errands before returning to the trials for a final ceremony. I rolled through a stop sign and a policeman pulled me over, giving me a ticket. *Doesn't he know that I just made the Olympic Games? I* remember thinking. *Why is he giving me a ticket right now?* My sense of entitlement was in full bloom already.

In my pride, I thought this officer should have known who I was. I thought I was owed something—in this instance, freedom from getting a ticket.

This sense of entitlement is a common affliction among elite athletes. And it's something I have to guard against carefully. When you're treated like a king during competitions, when you're stopped on the street for autographs, when people ask to have their pictures taken with you, it's easy to begin thinking that you deserve such recognition and praise. I have to constantly remind myself that every success and every accolade is a gift—one that I didn't earn. Yes, I worked hard, but I was born with my athletic abilities. God gave them to me so his name could be praised and not mine (which we will talk about later). When I lose sight of that, I begin to think I deserve to be treated as special and other people do not.

The Olympic Trials weren't the only major event in my life at that time. Several months before the 2008 trials, I began the decision-making process about my future. It was 2007, and I was a high school senior. The way I saw it, I had two choices: go professional with my diving or go to college. Thomas and I were wrestling with the same decision. We were having so much success that the professional route was a viable option. We could have enlisted enough sponsors to invest in us and support us in our competitive diving to make a good living for several years. That was certainly attractive to me, especially since I could see how that option would move me another step toward my goal of becoming rich and famous.

The fall of 2007, at the beginning of my senior year, I began making official recruiting visits to colleges. I was still seriously considering the professional option, but the recruiting trips gave me a chance to see different colleges, have fun, and taste the college lifestyle. What hedonistic, self-centered eighteen-year-old wouldn't want to do that?

I visited Auburn and Indiana. I had Ohio State lined up as well. Then one day I got a call from Adam Soldati, the diving coach at Purdue, who was interested in me coming to dive for him as a Purdue Boilermaker. Since Purdue was only an hour away from my home, I decided to make an unofficial visit to the campus to check it out and hear what Adam had to say.

My visit to Purdue was more influential than I had expected. I felt at home there. A few weeks later, Adam visited with my parents and me at our house. He laid everything out, explaining why he thought I should choose the NCAA route in general and Purdue specifically. Adam's wife, Kimiko, was familiar with my dilemma. She was a competitive diver who had gone professional after college and made some decent money, so she knew both worlds. As he made his case, Adam had to confront some immature thinking on my part. As I did with most things, I wanted the immediate satisfaction of becoming a professional athlete and tasting the riches that would appease me for the moment. I cared little about the long-term ramifications.

But Adam gently pointed out that the end to that life came quickly. He was wise and discerning and made a strong case for the collegiate path. Gradually, Adam and another diver on the Purdue team helped me see the wisdom of going to college. And Purdue seemed like the place I needed to be. I officially committed to going there in November 2007.

I still couldn't put my finger on what it was about Adam that I found so enticing, but he simply drew me in. His coaching style and the way he handled his athletes, both in and out of the pool, made me comfortable. I had little idea how large a role Adam would play in my life in the days ahead. I'm still amazed at how God was orchestrating things in my life to bring me to faith in him, even when I was completely uninterested in him.

CHAPTER 5

BETRAYING GOD

Y ou'd think I would have been ecstatic about officially making the Olympic team in both the individual and synchro events. This had been my all-consuming passion for more than a decade. It was what I had worked for, trained for, and sacrificed for. It was the pinnacle of my existence, and I was coming face-to-face with my god.

While I was elated, I didn't allow myself to get too excited about the achievement because the closer I came to my goal, the more my goal changed. No longer was I content just to make the Olympics. Now I had to move on to the next step: a medal. I wasn't able to fully experience the joy of accomplishing a dream because I was obsessed with attaining the next thing that was just out of my reach. USA Diving needed medals, so I was going to provide them.

The Beijing Olympics were one of the most hyped and anticipated Olympic events in a long time, even by the Olympics' standard. It was the first time China had hosted the Olympic Games, and the Chinese were going to make sure their country, often maligned for its human-rights violations, looked good. They certainly had a way of making an impression architecturally, from the Bird's Nest for the track-and-field events to the Water Cube where I would be competing.

The 2008 Olympics consumed so much of my life that I had been studying everything there was to know about them since 2004. I had followed the construction progress on a weekly basis. I knew exactly how the pool was going to look. I even knew what the medals were going to look like. When I arrived in Beijing, full of anticipation and excitement, everything looked exactly like what I had been seeing.

All the Olympic athletes were treated like royalty from the time we stepped off the plane. For our transportation, we had an Olympic lane on the freeway that was only for official Olympic use. Beijing's traffic is horrible, but we zoomed through it all in no time because we were Olympians. Everything dripped extravagance. *This*, I thought, *is exactly the kind of life I want. The eyes of the world are watching me. They're treating me like a king. I don't want this to stop.*

That royal treatment continued when it came time for our outfitting. Olympic athletes get a crazy amount of stuff, and for each Olympics the haul of goodies is different, depending on that year's sponsors. In Beijing, Team USA had rented out an entire building for the purpose of passing out the gear. Nike and Ralph Lauren were the chief sponsors, but other sponsors also provided a lot of stuff. I went into this building with a clipboard and moved from station to station, checking off everything I was given. Jackets. Polo shirts. T-shirts. Workout shorts. You get a whole wardrobe. You also get valuable things like a really nice watch and a ring. By the time you're finished, you leave with two huge suitcases (also gifts) full of goods; I had one Ralph Lauren suitcase and one Nike suitcase. You also have a duffel bag stuffed full. This is what I lived for at the time. I tried to find my satisfaction in stuff.

For the opening ceremony, the entire US team—all five hundred of us—met in the fencing hall. President George W. Bush addressed us, congratulating us on what we had achieved. That was the moment I felt like I was truly a part of the Olympic team, with little difference between me and some of my more famous teammates, such as Kobe Bryant, LeBron James, Michael Phelps, and others. I had seen these superstars for years on TV, and here I was walking right next to them, talking to them, feeling like I deserved the same acclaim.

As we walked to the Bird's Nest from the fencing hall,

the wait seemed endless. We were all drenched with sweat in our Ralph Lauren suits. We had to walk through a tiny white tunnel before entering the Bird's Nest, and the moment seemed to swell with expectation. The nerves. The anxiety. The realization that we were Olympians, and we were preparing to walk around the stadium in the parade of nations. Wow. What a feeling that was. We began chanting, "USA," and it echoed through the entire tunnel, reverberating off the walls and heightening our sense of excitement.

I wasn't a Christian at the time, but I still remember my heart being filled with gratitude that moment as we emerged into the stadium. It was sobering and humbling to be numbered with the world's greatest athletes as we heard the cheers going up for Team USA. I wept uncontrollably as I walked around the track and then into the stadium's center. I texted my dad, who was in attendance with the rest of my family, telling him how thankful I was. My parents had poured so much into me to make this dream of mine happen. They had sacrificed money and time. They had listened to me complain about my failures and celebrated with me in my successes. I had watched the Atlanta Olympics at seven years of age, and that scene of Team USA in the opening ceremony parade had impressed itself vividly on my memory. Here I stood, twelve years later, a part of it myself.

I returned to my room that night physically and emotionally exhausted. My sports psychologist had advised me to ride the Olympic roller coaster during the games, by which he meant I would experience highs and lows. While I could articulate that verbally, I wasn't sure how to do it in reality. The opening ceremony was clearly a high. But the next day, that jubilation was over. It was a nosedive, straight down. I had to turn around a couple of days later and compete on the Olympic stage. It was time to switch to game mode.

My first competition was the synchro with Thomas. We had medaled in so many competitions previously that we knew we could get on the podium if we dove like we were capable of diving. The event consisted of five dives, with eight teams participating. Thomas and I were extremely relaxed. We joked a lot to take the edge off on our way up the stairs to the platform. As we awaited our turn, I began to get focused. I put on my headphones and played a video game to get my mind off the competition. After our dive, we went to our coach to get some cues about what to do on the next one. And so it went, turn after turn, until all five dives were complete. The whole process took about forty-five minutes from start to finish—a pretty quick competition.

I didn't watch the scoreboard as we competed. I didn't know what scores we had received, what place we were in, anything at all. Thomas, however, was paying attention. After our fifth and final dive, I exited the pool knowing we had dived well and knowing that the outcome would likely be close. I looked at Thomas, and I could tell he was bummed. When I finally checked the scoreboard, I shared his disappointment. We had finished ten points away from the silver. Five points away from the bronze. Four points away from fourth place. A disheartening fifth-place finish.

The blow stung. I thought my performance had been amazing. I hadn't missed anything. Every twist, every flip, every entry had been on point. I expected us to get a medal. That wasn't the case. Of the eight best teams in the world diving in the Olympics, we weren't even in the top half. We had failed to deliver a medal for the United States in yet another diving event.

At the same time, I knew that I was not yet finished with the Beijing Olympics. My individual event in the 10-meter platform was still to come, days away and near the end of the games. I had won a bronze medal six months earlier in the same event at the same pool against the same divers. Ever confident, I did my best to put the failed synchro event behind me and focus instead on what came next. My glory and fame still hung there for the taking, and the good thing about it was that I wouldn't have to share it with anyone else.

The competition schedule left me with about ten days to kill before my individual event. Thomas and I spent a lot of time exploring the Olympic Village, where all the athletes are housed during the games. We went to the silk market in Beijing, where you can get a lot of stuff really cheap. We bought PlayStation Portable game systems and a ton of games, and I wasted hours in my room playing them. I attended a couple of the gymnastics events because I had friends on the women's team.

But mostly, when I wasn't training, I stuck to my room and tried to prepare myself mentally for the 10-meter competition. Even though my family was there, I saw them only a couple of times over the duration of the games. I was exceptionally irritable and short with them and anyone else I wrongly perceived to be an obstacle in my mental game.

That wasn't exactly new. I'd spent the previous four years pretty much being a jerk to everyone unless I had something to gain from them. I was the center of the universe, and people mattered only to the extent that they could meet a need of mine or deliver something of use to me. I regret now how poorly I treated people, and I am thankful that God has given me a heart that wants to serve and minister to others. At the time, though, doing that was the last thing on my mind.

Finally, after days of waiting, the time came for the 10-meter individual competition. I was hyped, focused, and confident as I went through my warm-up routine and prepared for the task ahead. Olympic medal, coming up.

My first dive, a forward three-and-a-half somersault pike, was subpar. My score of 64.50 came nowhere close to the scores in the 80s and 90s I'd need to contend seriously.

But I recovered from there, posting scores over the final five dives in the preliminary round that left me in sixth place at 481.70 points, plenty good enough to qualify for the semifinals.

Scores in each round begin fresh and don't carry over from previous rounds. In the semifinals, I improved from my first-round performance and finished fifth. Just some small improvements in the finals would get me to where I longed to be—on the medal stand. My confidence soared and I had little doubt that I was capable of making those necessary improvements.

But the reality was far from what I envisioned. After two dives in the final round, I was in fifth place, still within striking distance of a medal. I dropped to sixth place after my third dive. When I failed to move up after my next two dives, I was in seventh place with one dive left. I knew then that I wasn't going to medal. No way. No how. Game over.

My Olympic experience ended disastrously. I went completely short on the dive, meaning that instead of entering the water vertically, I came in at a horrible angle. Even now, I cringe when I see replays of that dive. I was trying to take in the experience, so I wasn't in my zone, and that humiliating dive was the result.

I finished in tenth place overall, a considerable distance away from what I was expecting. I tried to be strong and not show that it was affecting me, but the pain and the disappointment were excruciating. Even worse, I had to walk through the mixed zone, where athletes answer questions from the media immediately following the event. I remember a reporter asking me about the state of USA Diving with our failure to medal yet again.

"China didn't build their Great Wall in four years, so neither can we," I answered. "It's a process, and we can't expect to go into the games rebuilding everything that quickly."

Maybe it was an excuse, but it was also the truth. If you go in focusing on the results, then you'll rarely get the results you want. I learned that painful lesson that year. I don't know if it's true in all cases, but it certainly is in diving. If you're focusing on the podium, then you're not focusing on one dive at a time, which is what you should be doing. At the time, I was thinking only about medals, medals, medals. Or funding, funding, funding for USA Diving and myself. As a result, I didn't execute the dives the way I needed to in order to accomplish that goal. Focusing on the results is a recipe for failure. And that's what I did.

Shortly after the competition, USA Diving held a dinner party for the entire US team. I suffered through it as one of the worst experiences of my life. My family attended with me, but once we arrived, I checked out. The whole party was a somber occasion. I think everyone was bummed because, once again, we didn't win any medals in diving. But the sorrow may have been more painful for me. It was my fault we didn't win any medals. I was in the last event.

I could have delivered. I had done it before, and I should have been able to do it again.

Mentally drained, I couldn't put on a tough-guy face anymore. I still didn't let anyone see me cry, but I left the dinner party and locked myself in a bathroom stall, where all the heartache and disappointment came pouring out in a torrent of tears. My god had betrayed me. The one I had served for so long, the one I had worked for and sacrificed for, the one whose approval I so desperately sought, the one I was willing to do anything to appease had toyed with me and promised me something that it didn't deliver. It had beaten me down and crushed me in return for all I had given. Never in my life had I been so distraught.

Maybe you've been there, too, and have experienced something similar. Anything we create ourselves is not meant to carry the weight of our strongest desires and dreams. Anything we put our hope in, short of the Creator himself, will either crumble or fall short of the joy that God intended for us to have in him. That's why I was so crushed: I was placing my hope in the wrong place, and the only possible outcome was defeat and frustration.

I don't remember eating that night. I don't remember much about the dinner party. What I do remember is that wooden bathroom stall. I pounded the door with my fist, utterly and totally devastated.

I went back to the table, where my dad tried to console me. He told me how proud he was of me. But then another wave of despair would hit, and back to the bathroom I'd go. *Screw this*, I'd think to myself. I spent more time in the bathroom that night than I did at the party.

The closing ceremony came the next day. I had complained and groaned and moped and smoked so many cigarettes over the past day that I was able to put on a happy face and actually enjoy the event a little. My resolve had strengthened. I knew I had to get past this fiasco and set my face toward London. An Australian had beaten the seemingly invincible Chinese in the men's 10-meter, so that was my motivation and my catalyst to move forward and do what was necessary not just to medal in London but to win the gold. More desperately than ever, I wanted to be the savior of USA Diving.

I didn't even entertain the thought that I was the one who needed saving.

CHAPTER 6

CHAOS AT COLLEGE

School was never high on my priority list. I didn't enjoy many of the subjects, so I did only what I needed to do to get by. Had I applied myself, I easily could have been an A or B student. But in reality I was a B or C student who was more interested in being the funny and ornery kid in class than in actually learning. I was so silly and immature during my eighth-grade year that a teacher once told me, "You're going into high school. These high school kids are going to think you're a joke."

When I did get to high school, I was more concerned with being in the in-crowd than anything else, and I was terribly enslaved by my insecurities. I was consumed with what other people thought of me. I was consumed by how

I looked. I wanted everyone to like me, and I wanted to be the popular guy in school. I achieved some of that because of my athletic success, but it came at the expense of being totally preoccupied with myself and constantly worrying about what everybody else thought. For me, in that big suburban high school, social status was everything.

The older I got, the more school began to interfere with my training as an elite athlete. So during the second semester of my junior year, my parents, coach, and I decided that I'd stop attending high school and begin online schooling at home. That switch was a tremendous relief because I was so tired of the drama that came along with the life I was trying to live as the popular kid.

The homeschooling really weeded out a lot of the busy-work, solving another issue that had annoyed me in high school. From my perspective as an immature high school student, it seemed that teachers just gave us work to do because they were trying to keep us busy. But no more. The independent, online homeschooling suited my personality. I had an easily identifiable objective. For example, I knew I'd be done with a class after doing, say, eight assignments and taking two exams. I could see the end goal and the steps I'd need to take. Sometimes I would procrastinate on my work, but typically I did a good job of getting it done.

My training regimen was intense during my last couple of years of high school. I'd get up at 5:30 a.m. and spend half an hour on the elliptical before eating breakfast and heading to practice at 7:30 a.m. We'd do two hours of dry-land work and then take a two-hour break. Sometimes I'd spend that break doing my schoolwork (which was really the purpose of that break), but much of the time I'd spend goofing off with my teammates. Then, in the afternoons, I did work in the pool, then weight training or Pilates, then ballet, which helped with strength and flexibility. We were working out nonstop on a daily basis. It was difficult, but I was so obsessed with my body image and the way I looked that I was willing to suffer through it. My body would collapse if I tried to train like that now.

As a young diver, though, I completely bought in to the mind-set that my appearance meant everything—especially in my sport, where the judging is based on how a dive looks and how you present yourself. If you look like you're out of shape, it looks like you don't care. Your scores may suffer because of it. It's easy to see that the best competitors at meets are in tip-top shape, and it's easy to start comparing yourself to others. Divers can become obsessed with being the fittest, strongest, skinniest, most cut athlete out there, and I was no different. That's one reason I was motivated to work so hard.

After practicing and training, I'd usually get home about four thirty in the afternoon. Then I would have the rest of the day to eat, do homework, or hang out with my friends or family. For me, homeschooling was much easier than the traditional schooling. I think it helped prepare me for college because it taught me to learn independently. I still went back to my old high school for proms and dances, but I loved the year and a half I spent as a homeschool student. When it came time for me to go to college, I felt adequately prepared. I never felt like the dumb kid in class, but I also didn't feel like I was the smartest. I was basically an average student.

I started my college freshman year a few days late because of the Beijing Olympics. My first classes began on a Monday, but I didn't get back from Beijing until Tuesday. I landed at about 3:00 p.m. that day, and by 6:00 p.m. I had my car packed up and ready to go. I left home at 4:00 a.m. on Wednesday to head to my first class at 7:30 a.m. Though the Beijing experience was a major disappointment, I still was looking forward to college. Moving there and starting fresh helped temper the sadness I was feeling, even if that tempering was short-lived.

In a way, going to college was humbling for me, at least at first. I was in a completely new environment with people who didn't know me, so I didn't conduct myself with my usual cockiness and swagger. In my very first class (a speech class), my instructor asked me where I was during the previous session I had missed. I told him I was overseas. He kept digging, so I told him I was competing overseas. He probed further, so I finally told him I was at the Olympics. I was pleased with myself for being humble enough not to come right out and trumpet the fact that I was an Olympian. At the same time, I was glad he kept asking.

It's difficult to explain exactly how I wanted people to see me. I didn't want to be treated differently because I was an elite athlete and an Olympian. But I also wanted them to know that I was. Maybe that sounds silly, but I think that's human nature. At the end of the day, we want everything to be about us. When it fed my desire to be seen and recognized, I wanted it. When it didn't serve that purpose, I wanted to be more anonymous. I wanted to have control over my circumstances to serve my own felt needs in the moment.

That speech class turned out to be more difficult than I'd expected. It should have been easy because I had spoken in front of people before. But I was constantly nervous. For my second speech, I was on edge. I wanted to feel more comfortable in my presentation so much that I actually thought about pounding some beers before giving my speech to take the edge off and make me loose. But I didn't follow through for a couple reasons: one, I feared it would mess me up for the rest of the day; and two, it was seven thirty in the morning.

Going away to college was also a freeing experience for me. I loved my parents, but now I didn't have to tell anyone where I was going or when I'd be home. I had a social life for once because I wasn't training all the time. College allowed me to be somewhat normal.

As an NCAA Division I athlete, I was required to spend time at Purdue's "study tables" for a certain number of hours every week until I proved I no longer needed them. The study tables are located in a complex Purdue built specifically for athletes, where they scan in, pick a seat at a table or desk, spend their allotted time studying, and then scan out. That system monitors the amount of time you spend studying. If your grade point average is above 2.5, you don't have to go to the study tables. If it's under 2.5, you have to spend five to ten hours a week there. Tutors are on call to help with several subjects. If you need help with a particular class, you just step outside the room where you are studying and go to see a tutor. I had a tutor in math, because I hate math.

In addition to a regular academic advisor, all athletes at Purdue had an athletic academic advisor. I met with mine on a weekly basis, letting her know what my assignments were and how I was doing in my classes. Her job was to make sure I was staying on task. As I said, for the most part, I was an average student. My biggest challenge that year was time management. I struggled at first with learning how to balance my coursework with my competition schedule, but I made strides the longer I was at school. The key for me was not procrastinating on my work and keeping open channels of communication with my professors.

Dorm life at Purdue was a blast. When I got to my room and met my roommate, Thomas Wilson, I was pleased because it was clear he wanted to be the cool guy, just like I did. I noticed vomit on the chair from the night before, so Thomas had certainly jumped into the party lifestyle quickly. As I got to know him better, though, I discovered something about him that was at odds with his party-guy image. He'd had some Christian influences in his life, and he professed to be a believer. I didn't know what that meant at the time, but he had a lot of Bibles and other Christian knick-knacks on his shelf. This component to his life made me a bit curious but nothing more. I didn't want to go to his church. I didn't want to go to Fellowship of Christian Athletes with him. I was fine, thanks.

Thomas and I ended up being great friends and partners in crime. We behaved like juveniles in the dorms, ripping stuff off the wall, stealing people's towels in the showers, whatever we could do for fun. Of course, sin typically is fun for a season. And for me, that sin was extremely fun.

Thomas, though he professed to be a Christian, often didn't live his life in a way that portrayed Christ when he was a freshman. But when he came back for his sophomore year, he had thoroughly changed. Now that I have the eyes to see it, it's clear he had been redeemed from the life he was living. He had decided to be faithful in following Christ. That was awful for me because I wanted the room-mate I'd had my freshman year. I wanted the Thomas who would drink with me and live that crazy college lifestyle with me. But that wasn't him anymore. We grew apart for the time being, but God had a purpose for him in my life that I couldn't yet see.

Of course, I wasn't at Purdue to raise Cain in the dorms and to party on the weekends, though I did plenty of both. I was at Purdue to be an NCAA Division I diver. Once I got back from Beijing, I was supposed to take a couple of weeks off, but I was so excited to get going that I was back at it after a week. Since I had been on the world stage, NCAA wasn't that big of a deal for me. I'd go through dry spells, but typically I won every competition, whether it was the 1-meter, the 3-meter, or the platform. On rare occasions I finished second, but first place was the norm.

Providing unintentional comic relief for my team seemed to be another of my responsibilities. During one of my first competitions, I failed a dive on the 1-meter. That means I didn't complete the dive and scored a zero. I might have scored higher if I had done a cannonball instead. I came out of the dive and landed like an idiot, "stapling" the water. That's where your hands and your feet hit the water at about the same time. Not good. The following weekend, I failed another dive. The team loved it. It was humiliating to me, but it was highly amusing to my teammates.

We used a video system called Dartfish that recorded all our dives and allowed us to go back, play the dives in slow motion, and analyze them. Those two failed dives, of course, were in there. My teammates loved watching those dives and laughing mercilessly at my expense. At first it was funny, since I was an Olympian and shouldn't have been doing dives like that. But then it got to be like a broken record. I thought, *Okay, guys, just stop. Yeah, we've seen this a hundred times.*

With those early failed dives out of my system, I started winning again. At Big Ten competitions, I won Big Ten Diver of the Week regularly, consistently sweeping all three diving events—the 1-meter and 3-meter springboard and the 10-meter platform. At the NCAA diving championships held at Texas A&M, I finished second in the 1-meter but then took both the 3-meter and the 10-meter titles. Purdue named me its Athlete of the Year as a freshman. The university's alumni magazine even did a cover story on me that year, which pumped me up even more:

> Much more than a freshman phenom, Boudia possessed such global exposure that some were surprised he opted to attend Purdue in the first place. To think of him as a blue-chip recruit might be akin to wondering how Kobe and LeBron (two famous first names in the National Basketball Association) would have fared in college hoops. By 18 years of age, Boudia was already a world-class athlete near the top of his game. He was named 2008 USA Diving Athlete of the Year. From 2006 through 2008, Boudia and Thomas Finchum,

his partner in the synchronized 10-meter platform, medaled in 14 international events, including 10 consecutive events. Prior to that, in 2004, before either athlete could legally drive, they dove to a third place finish at the Olympic Trials in St. Louis. Last summer, the duo finished fifth in the event in Beijing, less than five points away from a bronze medal.[1]

I was the big man on campus and was living the dream. Not all the athletes at Purdue knew me, but I thought they should because of what I had accomplished. And I did it all despite putting on some weight because of my drinking and being undisciplined outside the pool. Oh, I did the workouts. I lifted the weights and did what Adam Soldati and my weight coach told me to do. I performed what was required of me in the pool. Except for weight training, my training outside of the pool was a different story.

I wasn't taking care of my body or eating well. At the dorms, I ate whatever I felt like eating. I drank with friends just about every weekend. I wanted to be part of the social world that surrounded those weekend parties. Occasionally I'd even get talked into skipping my Friday-morning class after partying with a fraternity on a Thursday night. I didn't need much convincing. I knew I still had to perform in the classroom, but I also knew how much class I could miss without putting me in jeopardy of getting a D or an F.

I fully embraced the party lifestyle, regardless of its

effects on my health and my obligations at the school. I had stopped smoking marijuana in high school because it was hurting my body, and I knew I could get drug tested. Purdue even tested us at the beginning of my freshman year. But a few weeks later some friends and I decided we wanted to smoke. I hadn't done it in years, but that Sunday night, I got high. I figured I was okay and that we wouldn't be tested again anytime soon.

Imagine my alarm the next day in practice when they announced a random drug test. I was freaking out. A few of my teammates had gotten high with me, so I knew they were in trouble as well. After practice, I stood in the shower and tried to drink as much of the shower water as I could to dilute my urine. The effort proved fruitless, and I failed the test. I was put on a probation schedule, meaning I was tested periodically throughout that year until I could prove that I wasn't smoking marijuana.

Now that I can look back at it, I see that incident as evidence of Galatians 6:7–8: "Do not be deceived: God is not mocked, for whatever one sows, that will he also reap. For the one who sows to his own flesh will from the flesh reap corruption, but the one who sows to the Spirit will from the Spirit reap eternal life." I did something stupid and was sowing to my own flesh. So I reaped the consequences of that action. God allowed me to reap those consequences not because he didn't like me but because he knew what I needed.

Testing positive was an eye-opener for me, and it was my first strike with Adam. I was terrified of how he would respond. I was expecting a good tongue-lashing and lecturing, but that's not what Adam did. He didn't point his finger at me and tell me I was a bad kid. Instead, he handled it compassionately, extending grace to me and giving me what I didn't deserve. He also told me not to let it happen again.

Letting Adam down was traumatizing. I never want to let my coach down. So I made a point not to get in trouble with the authorities again. The episode didn't change my heart, but it did serve to modify my external behavior for a while.

My success in diving at Purdue helped to soften the blow from Beijing, but I continued to be more and more consumed with myself. My highs were high and my lows were low. I lived by how I felt. When I was annoyed, everyone was annoying to me. When I was happy, everyone was delightful to me. My heart was on my sleeve, and people could tell exactly what was going on in my life by how I acted toward them.

Winning at the collegiate level provided some temporary, though fleeting, satisfaction. I'd think, *I won Big Ten Athlete of the Week again? Oh, sweet!* Then the certificate went in the locker with the rest of them, and that was that. I was pleased with how I was performing, but being a successful NCAA diver was not the ultimate goal. It was a stepping-stone toward winning an Olympic gold medal. That dream was still intact, even after Beijing.

My time in the NCAA was an important and pivotal step in my life. It validated my decision to go to college instead of turning professional. As a college diver, I was competing almost every single weekend—thirty or forty times a year. Had I turned professional, I would have been competing only about ten or fifteen times a year. That volume of competitions helped me tweak my routine and really learn how to compete as an athlete. It also made me more comfortable in high-stakes competitions because I had walked through the scenario so many times before. The NCAA provided a safe place for me to develop and hone my mental game.

While I continued to focus on my gold-medal goal, I encountered a different mind-set in Adam's coaching. He slowly began to teach me exactly what it meant to train and have a goal, but he emphasized how important it was to be process oriented instead of results oriented. Adam always said it was not his job to make a diver a champion, but to create an environment where a champion can be made. He did just that. He created an environment where I could succeed and get to an even higher level. But he wasn't going to promise to make me a champion. It was all up to me.

It took me a while to get used to that approach because

I was so focused on winning everything. The gold medal at the Olympics was my outcome goal. Now, how would I do that? Adam brought back to life the early counseling I'd gotten from my sports psychologist. Over time, I had abandoned process thinking, but he encouraged me to value the process and the journey to the goal, not just the goal itself. He also applied a lot of biblical principles in his coaching—principles that I had no idea were biblical.

For example, Adam talks about the "principle of the path," telling his athletes that they get to choose their path, but they don't get to choose the destination. Their direction determines where they end up, not their intentions.[2] When athletes choose to be lazy and not complete their assignments, they are choosing a path of destruction that will lead to poor grades and possibly getting kicked out of school. When they choose to do hard things, they are setting themselves up for success. That's an example straight from Deuteronomy 30:19: "I call heaven and earth to witness against you today, that I have set before you life and death, blessing and curse. Therefore choose life, that you and your offspring may live." I wanted nothing to do with God at the time, yet Adam was laying a foundation for that relationship without preaching at me.

At the end of my freshman year I decided I wanted to stay at Purdue and train with Adam and the rest of the team over the summer. Purdue had an accelerated term called a Maymester, so I enrolled in a class and moved into an apartment with some friends. But the class was difficult and the training regimen was exhausting. I grew tired of the routine after several weeks; I think I attended two class sessions before I dropped out. It was too much at the time. So I went to Adam and told him that I wanted to move back home and train with my old coach during the summer. He was fine with that, and I moved out of the apartment about three days after moving in and headed home to Noblesville. The summer launched me even further into despair.

CHAPTER 7

REDEMPTION

I spent most of my time that summer preparing for the 2009 World Aquatics Championships in Rome in July. I finished sixth in the 10-meter platform, but Thomas Finchum and I placed second in the 10-meter synchro. That was an encouraging result, and it made me feel that I was continuing on track for the 2012 Olympics in London, where I wanted nothing less than gold.

In addition to my training, I also spent a good amount of time that summer drinking. One of the divers on the US women's team trained in Indianapolis, and I was good friends with her older brother. We reconnected that summer and hung out constantly. He was a big drinker. So, naturally, I joined right in. After the world championships,

I spent several days in Florida with his family on vacation. We ate, we slept, we hung out with the family, we played games, and we drank. A lot. I did it to escape my reality, and I did it to pursue pleasure.

It gave me anything but. My life was increasingly characterized by frustration and emptiness. Here I was, pursuing all these hedonistic pleasures. I was a world-class athlete on the path to make it big in London. I was one of the top athletes at a major Division I university. I was young and seemed to have life by the tail, as the saying goes. *All these things should satisfy me*, I thought. *I ought to be happy.* But it all felt empty, void, and vain. As the preacher says in Ecclesiastes, "Vanity of vanities . . . all is vanity" (1:2). That's what I started to feel that summer, and those feelings would only intensify in the days ahead.

After that vacation, it was time to move back to Purdue for my sophomore year. I lived off campus that year in a house with four other guys, one of whom was my freshman roommate, Thomas Wilson. My feelings of hopelessness and emptiness vanished for a while, because this living arrangement was something new, and I rode the high that came along with it. I was always craving something new, different, and exciting, but there's a difference between enjoying the novelty and looking to it for fulfillment. Once I found something different, I was all in, trying to suck every last drop of happiness and pleasure out of it that I could, but I got bored easily when the newness wore off.

I loved the new setup. Well, I loved everything except for what was going on with Thomas. He had attended a conference with his girlfriend that summer and had encountered God in a powerful way. Though he had been a professed Christian for a few years, he hadn't been consistently living a faithful Christian life. All that changed after he came back as a sophomore. While my other roommates and I hosted parties regularly at our house, Thomas didn't participate anymore. He didn't drink himself silly anymore. He was definitely different.

Although his changed life was annoying, it didn't mean much to me. I had other friends to party with. And the first few weeks of the semester, we did a lot of that. But again, the newness and excitement of that didn't last. Just like I had a few weeks before, I began to tire of the routine, the sameness, the hopelessness and emptiness that I kept feeling. I even got sick of diving and kicked around the idea of quitting. It all came crashing down in a hurry, eventually reaching a breaking point on a Saturday in September.

For several days prior to that, I had entertained suicidal thoughts. My consistent frame of mind was, *This is so dumb. What's the point of this life?* I was constantly consumed with thoughts of not wanting to be here on this earth anymore. I never went so far as to figure out a plan of action and write a note, but suicide wasn't off the table as an option for me. I couldn't figure out how to reconcile the conflicts in my mind. The things that were supposed to bring me happiness—the worldly success, the fleshly indulgences—were having the opposite effect, driving me to despair rather than delight. And if my continued pursuit of such pleasures was only going to lead to more of the same result, I didn't know how long I could handle that. I was obsessed with myself, and yet I hated myself for it.

Though I never seriously considered suicide as an option, the thoughts did pop into my mind periodically because I wanted what was easy. At times, forgetting everything seemed like the easiest option. Just total nothingness. I think that's a common mind-set, especially among teenagers, who think that ending their pain and despair by taking their own lives is the easy way out. In reality, suicide doesn't end that pain and despair. It simply transfers it to friends and family left behind who suffer tremendously in suicide's aftermath. If you're one of those considering suicide to end your problems, I plead with you to go to someone for help and reconsider. There is no problem so big that suicide is the proper answer. It doesn't solve anything.

My commitment to stop smoking probably didn't help my outlook on life. I had wanted to stop for some time, figuring that by my own self-will and determination I could kick the habit. I'd gone a week without a cigarette prior to that pivotal Saturday, and my skin was crawling. That was the longest I had gone without a cigarette since I started smoking at fifteen. I was extremely vulnerable and irritable. It's clear now that the Lord used that vulnerability to say, *All right, David. I'm going to knock you on your face. It's time to see that you're not God.*

That's what he did on Saturday, September 26. It was a big day on the Purdue campus, with the Purdue Boilermakers set to take on Notre Dame in a night football game. Purdue never played at night. In fact, Ross-Ade Stadium doesn't even have permanent lights, so they bring in temporary lighting for major events. And a game against Notre Dame certainly qualified. Located just a couple of hours down the road from West Lafayette, the Fighting Irish are one of Purdue's biggest rivals.

Everyone was pumped for the game. My summer drinking buddy went to Notre Dame, so he came to town for the game. The tailgating started early and went on all day long, and I was a little buzzed by the afternoon. I wasn't drunk, but a couple of hours before game time, I felt I needed a nap so I could be ready when kickoff came.

I returned to my room from the tailgate parties and fell asleep. When I woke up, something had changed dramatically. It felt like someone had hit me over the head. Nothing made sense to me whatsoever, and I felt emptier than I had in my entire life. My Notre Dame friend came up to try to corral me out of bed and get me going. I yelled at him to leave me alone and to not come into my room under any circumstances.

I sat there looking at an orange wall in my room, think-ing that life was pointless. The suicidal thoughts returned, and I didn't know what else to do. I was desperate for relief from my hopeless existence. I wanted freedom from my enslavement to the drinking and smoking. I thought this life was pointless, and I wanted it to be over. What I didn't know was that life was just about to begin.

I texted a diving teammate, Ashley Karnes (now Ashley Karshen). Ashley used to party right alongside me, drink-ing heavily like me. But recently, I hadn't seen her do that. I respected her, so I told her what was going on with me and asked her what I should do. She replied along the lines of, "I know this probably doesn't make sense, but this is maybe a cool stage you're in right now." *Cool? Does she have any idea what I'm going through?* "Cool" is not how I would describe it. She encouraged me to text my coach, Adam, and be transparent with him. I was willing to try anything, so that's what I did. He didn't reply immediately, but when he did, he told me he'd love for me to come over the next day and visit with him and his wife, Kimiko. I didn't leave my room the rest of the night. I tried to go back to sleep until the morning. All I knew was that I was eager to go to Adam's house so he could fix my problems.

Of course I knew Adam Soldati well, since he was my coach. I respected him tremendously. He and Kimiko seemed to have it all together. Their lives were ordered and peaceful. Their family was happy. The next day passed slowly until my appointment with them. I went to the mall to pass the time, hoping that maybe spending some money would bring me some relief. I didn't know exactly what they were going to talk to me about. Kimiko had been an Olympic diver herself, so I expected they would discuss what I was experiencing post-Olympics. I hoped they would tell me that I was normal, that every Olympic athlete went through these struggles, and it was all going to be okay: "Just give it some time, David, and you'll be fine."

All that would have been nice. But instead, they did something far better—something I was not expecting in the least.

I arrived at their house and sat down with them in the living room. Adam and Kimiko didn't need to engage in small talk. They already knew how I was doing. They began our talk by helping me see what I was chasing and where I was placing my hope. They understood the chaos, the pain, and the destruction in my life. They knew, because they had been there themselves. Kimiko's life, especially, was almost a carbon copy of my own. She had grown up in a strong moral home, but not a religious one. Her dad worked and her mom stayed home, and they had a stable, traditional family like mine. Sports consumed her life when she was younger, and her identity was completely wrapped up in athletics. Gymnastics was her first love, but she later switched to diving when an injury ended her gymnastics dreams. It's almost uncanny how parallel our lives were.

She and Adam met while they were students at Indiana University. Kimiko had transferred to IU from Colorado State University, and Adam had transferred from a junior college in California. Like Kimiko, Adam grew up with sports as the focal point of his life—baseball, football, basketball, swimming. He got into diving late but showed a lot of promise. As he was finishing his two years at junior college and deciding where to continue his education, he did a search for schools with diving programs and business schools. He found 112 options, so he wrote a letter and sent it to all 112 schools. Indiana was where he ended up.

After they were married and had finished college, life changed drastically for Adam and Kimiko. They grew weary, as I did, of chasing after things that didn't satisfy them. They explained to me that the loneliness and despair I was feeling was a result of misplaced hope. My pursuit of joy, satisfaction, and wholeness was a good thing, they said—a drive that was given to me by God. But I was looking for those things in the wrong places.

Rather than pursuing God and being satisfied in him, I was looking for fulfillment in the things God had made, and those creations were never meant to satisfy. Only God himself could fill that role. As God said to the prophet Jeremiah, "My people have committed two evils: they have forsaken me, the fountain of living waters, and hewed out cisterns for themselves, broken cisterns that can hold no water" (Jeremiah 2:13).

That's what I had done and what my whole life had been about. In chasing fame, pleasure, popularity, and whatever else I wanted in the moment, I was placing my trust in things that would never stop my thirst. And the cycle never ended. Even when my pursuits proved hollow, I kept going back to them again and again, expecting a different result. But the "cisterns" kept breaking, time after time.

Adam and Kimiko probed what I believed about God and why I made the decisions I had been making with my life. Adam gently pointed out that given my struggles, the way I had been living didn't seem to be working out too well. He was absolutely right. Living for myself and my own pleasures had gotten me nowhere fast. Here I was, a young man in the prime of life, with an immense amount of success already to my credit. Lots of people would have traded places with me without a second thought. And yet I was miserable and utterly disenchanted with life. God had given me that hunger and thirst for satisfaction that could only be found in a relationship with him.

They asked me about heaven and if I believed I would go there when I died.

"Well, yeah," I responded. "Of course I will, because I'm a pretty good person."

My hubris obviously knew no bounds. Here my life was in tatters, I was arrogant and self-centered, a jerk to those around me, a boozer and a potty-mouth, and I thought I was a pretty good person. After all, I hadn't killed anyone, right?

Then Adam and Kimiko began sharing a message that changed my life—a message that gave me hope, freedom, and purpose. It was the gospel, the "good news" about Jesus Christ and what he had done for me. Although I had grown up going to church, I thought God was kind of a buzzkill. I was taught that if I followed some basic rules, did what I was supposed to do, and lived a good life, that everything would be okay. I even would have considered myself a Christian, though I didn't understand what that meant. In reality, I was not a Christian at all. I had never had a personal encounter with Jesus Christ, nor had I ever addressed my rebellion against him.

My life was indeed a rebellion against God. Adam and Kimiko talked to me for the first time about sin. I honestly don't think I knew what sin was at the time. We hate that word, *sin*. We toss it around like it's something someone else does, and if we do sin, it's only a little sin. No big deal. They opened the Bible and shared verses like, "All have sinned and fall short of the glory of God" (Romans 8:23). They explained sin as a violation against a God who doesn't just expect my best but demands perfection. If he is perfect, if he is holy, he demands that perfection in us. Being a "good" person doesn't cut it. Living a good life isn't enough. When you're trying to be pleasing to a holy God, perfection is the only way. And the penalty for not meeting that standard, the consequence for my sin, is death. As Romans 6:23 says, "The wages of sin is death."

That was pretty alarming. After all, I knew I wasn't perfect. There was no way I could be good enough to earn God's favor. But why did I need to earn his favor? Well, since God was my creator and the sovereign king of the universe, I was accountable to him. My personal problems, then, were not a result of me simply failing to live the kind of life I should. I wasn't a victim of bad circumstances. I wasn't a victim of not finding the right thing to fulfill me. I wasn't a victim of others robbing my joy from me. I wasn't a victim of bad luck. My problems were a direct result of sin and rebellion against God himself. I alone was responsible for my sin, not anybody else. Though I was accountable to him, I had set myself up as God instead. I wanted to be in control. I wanted to do what I wanted. I wanted to be the one people praised and adored.

But God knows that this type of self-centered life leads only to misery, despair, and separation from him. Because of his love, he was stepping into my life at that moment and saying, *No more. This will not continue.* God's grace was telling me, through the words of Adam and Kimiko and the scriptures they shared with me, that my insistence on being God was creating my misery.

That message can sound hopeless and terrifying at first. And it did. After all, if God was holy and I was not, and if I was in a dreadful state of rebellion against the rightful king who deserved and demanded my allegiance, what hope was there for me?

That's where the good news comes in. God knew that I couldn't meet his standard of perfection. Remember what Romans 6:23 says, that the wages of sin is death? That verse goes on to offer life-changing hope: "but the free gift of God is eternal life in Christ Jesus our Lord." Adam and Kimiko explained that though I had rebelled against him, the Lord loved me and had provided a means of salvation for me in the midst of my rebellion. What a thought!

They told me that God demonstrated that love by giving us his Son, Jesus Christ. Jesus was God himself who became a man. He lived a life without sin. He died a gruesome death on the cross to take my sin and my rebellion upon himself and face God's wrath against it for me. He died for my past, present, and future sin by taking the punishment I deserved. He bore it himself so I didn't have to bear it. There was a way out of the sin that was crushing me. He conquered sin and death by rising from the dead. The Bible says that all who believe in that message and turn to Christ in repentance and faith are adopted as God's children (John 1:12). Even after all my mistakes, God made a way for me to be his child.

Whoa. It sounded so heavy and complex. What did it all mean? For one, my love for success, for wealth, and for myself was rebellion against God that deserved God's wrath. I had no way to earn my way back into God's favor. No wonder I felt like my life was a dead end. Without Jesus, it was. But God took care of that for me by providing Christ to pay for my sin. Jesus gave me the perfection I needed to stand before God without fault and without blemish. Because Jesus was fully man, he understood all the temptations that are common to man. Because he was God, he endured those temptations without succumbing to them (Hebrews 4:15). He lived a life free from the sin and rebellion that characterize all our lives. Free from the sin that had brought me so low.

When he died on the cross, because he had no sin of his own for God to punish, he assumed the punishment for *my* sin instead. Instead of me dying, Jesus died. He took the punishment I deserved, and he gave me *his* righteousness, which I was lacking. I couldn't earn that righteousness myself, but Christ offers it as a gift.

Adam and Kimiko explained that when we accept what Christ has done for us, we acknowledge our sin. We own up to the fact that we do actually rebel against him. We repent of that sin, telling God that we don't want to continue living in rebellion. When we do that, trusting in Jesus' sacrifice on our behalf, God offers us forgiveness. This allows us to enter his presence both here on earth and in eternity to come. Accepting Christ into our lives isn't only about going to heaven but experiencing a fullness in life on earth by faithfully walking with him every day. It's an unimaginably life-changing gift.

Adam and Kimiko spelled all this out for me, opening the Scriptures and telling me what the purpose of the cross was and what Christianity was all about. As I sat in their rocking chair listening to them talk, it was as if plugs popped out of my ears. In the book of Acts, after Paul's conversion, a man named Ananias came and laid his hands on a blind Paul, and something like scales fell from his eyes, allowing him to see again (9:18). That's what it was like for me. Rather than being turned off by what they were saying, I was receptive to it. My heart seemed to spring to life inside me. For the first time ever, I could see the hope in Christ. I felt a tremendous weight lift off my shoulders.

I'm not sure I was actually converted that night, because I don't think I fully understood what the gospel meant. But it didn't take long. I normally don't like reading, but that week I read more than I've read my entire life, trying to learn what this Jesus thing was all about. *The Cross Centered Life* by C. J. Mahaney was a huge help, and I still use that book today when I encounter new believers. I still have the e-mails Kimiko and I exchanged in the days after my first meeting with them. The very next day, she told me that Adam would get me a Bible that I could use temporarily until I got my own. "Until then, feel free to write, mark, highlight, underline whatever in the one he gives you," she told me.

She told me to read the book of John. I was so uninformed about the Bible that she had to tell me that it was a book in the New Testament in the back half of the Bible. It's a book about the life and death of Christ, she said, and John gives his reason for writing it in John 20:31. "These are written so that you may believe that Jesus is the Christ, the Son of God, and that by believing you may have life in his name."

Life. What a beautiful word. For so long I had lived without any kind of meaning or purpose. An aimless existence, flitting along from one temporary pleasure to the next. I grew increasingly disenchanted with the meaninglessness of it, but here I encountered a message that was life-giving.

Kimiko asked me to read the first five chapters of John and make notes about whatever popped out to me and write down any questions I had. She encouraged me not to worry if I didn't understand something but to keep reading. She also shared some verses with me that she thought pertained to my specific situation. I marveled at how these words from Scripture spoke so explicitly to me. For example, John 6:35: "Jesus said to them, 'I am the bread of life; whoever comes to me shall not hunger, and whoever believes in me shall never thirst.'" There's Acts 4:12, which talks about Jesus: "And there is salvation in no one else, for there is no other name under heaven given among men by which we must be saved."

She told me that God would never leave me or forsake me (Deuteronomy 31:6), and that she and Adam were praying for me. I used to roll my eyes at Bible verses or the idea that someone was praying for me. Now, however, I was craving it. The next Sunday I went with the Soldatis to church—Faith Church in Lafayette. Church had never played much of a role in my adult life. About the only time I went was if I had a competition coming up, and I thought attending church might somehow cause God to help me win. But now I was enthralled. I paid attention during the sermon, and I began to understand some of what the pastor said. I didn't fall asleep in my seat. My heart leaped for joy when the Soldatis dropped me off at home after the service and said they'd be going again that night.

"You're going back to church again?" I asked in astonishment. "Yeah, I'd love to go with you."

Church twice in one day? The old me would rather have done anything else. The new me—the one in whose heart God was doing a work of grace and redemption—couldn't get enough.

I met with Adam and Kimiko regularly in the weeks that followed, and my roommate Thomas often came along. The truths they taught us were exhilarating and refreshing.

I don't remember a specific time when I actually became a believer, a follower of Christ. It was more of a process than it was a single, life-changing moment. But I do remember lying in bed one night weeping because of how much I loved the Lord. Seriously. I understood my sinfulness and how much forgiveness God had extended to me. The David Boudia who had been so consumed with his fame and happiness was now in tears because of his love for Jesus. That is radical.

Within three months after they shared the gospel with me, I was ready to be baptized. Baptism is an outward expression of what has already taken place in the life of a Christian. There's nothing magical or saving in the act of baptism itself, but it does serve as a picture and a symbol to others. I knew what it meant to have a relationship with Christ and why I needed a relationship with him, and I was ready to make that profession of faith public.

This new life caused immediate and considerable changes in my behavior. My speech changed dramatically because I understood that dropping F-bombs (like I did regularly for years) did not glorify God. I stopped being as judgmental toward others. I used to always say what was on my mind. If I didn't like someone, I'd tell them directly that I didn't like them and explain exactly why. If someone annoyed me, I'd tell them why they were annoying me. But my new heart made me different. My desires were transformed, and they continue to be transformed.

Now, that's not to say I became perfect or sinless. That's not what happens when you become a Christian. We live in a fallen world—a world that is under God's curse because of our sin (Genesis 3). And our nature is still sinful. Though my desires changed, for the most part, and several things in my life became different, that didn't excuse me from doing battle with sin. I do battle on a daily and hourly basis, as every believer does. Some want you to think that it's possible to achieve perfection in this life, but that's not what Scripture teaches (1 John 1:8–10).

Although I didn't become perfect, I did become different. And people began to notice. My teammates at Purdue, for example, knew that something was different because I wasn't hanging out with them nonstop anymore. I still wanted to be friends with them, so I was often the designated driver at their parties for a few months. One night when I picked up one of my teammates, she heard something strange on my radio. It was K-LOVE, a Christian radio station. Before becoming a Christian, I didn't even know stations like that existed. But now, with a new heart, that's what I wanted to hear.

"Why are you listening to that?" she asked.

That's when it hit me that being different was going to have lasting implications, and that was a difficult realization. I knew if I was going to live for Christ, then friendships with my teammates would likely suffer. Not necessarily because I didn't want to be with them (though that was sometimes the case), but because they wouldn't want to be with me. While that transition of losing friends was troubling, I knew that God was calling me to something better. Something deeper. The Bible says that "friendship with the world is enmity with God" (James 4:4). I wanted friendship with God more than anything else, even if it cost me friendship with the world. That's not to say that I was suddenly better and holier than my old friends and wanted nothing to do with them. Not at all. It just meant that my desires and interests were no longer in sync with those of many of my old friends.

In addition to my teammates and friends, my sisters also were quick to pick up on how I had changed. A few weeks after my initial meeting with the Soldatis, my sister Shauni was going through a struggle eerily similar to the one I had faced. She played collegiate soccer at the University of Southern Indiana, and her senior season had ended. Just as diving was a major part of who I was as a person, soccer was a major part of Shauni. My older sister Shaila and I were driving down to Evansville to visit with Shauni, and on the way down, I remember asking Shaila if I could listen to a sermon.

Shaila had to wonder what in the world had happened to her brother.

Staying at Shauni's place, my sisters slept on the bed

while I slept on the floor. I took my Bible out and began reading it. They thought that something was different about me—that I was weird. We went to a fair called Fall Festival with carnival rides, fried foods, and people from all walks of life. I remember telling Shauni how difficult it was for me to be in that environment because it was hard for me not to judge the people I was looking at for a variety of reasons. Formerly, I would have been quick to poke fun at so many people who were out of shape and didn't care a bit how they looked. But now, for the first time, I was battling against that temptation to be so judgmental. While a sense of superiority to others certainly isn't godly, that's a statement I never would have made before. Later that night, I asked Shauni, "If you were to die tonight, would you go to heaven or hell?"

She was uncomfortable with the question, to say the least, and she gave a similar answer to the one I had given Adam and Kimiko. I challenged her on her response, though I didn't know enough at the time to go much deeper. But in the weeks ahead, as she struggled with the end of her soccer career, Shauni saw my life changing considerably. I had more joy and had put aside my old lifestyle. I told her during her depression that there were answers for her, and I encouraged her to come up and visit with Adam and Kimiko herself.

By God's grace, just weeks after my own conversion, both Shauni and Shaila made professions of faith in Christ, thanks in large part to the influence of Adam and Kimiko. The Lord's moving was becoming a family affair. I remember Thanksgiving and Christmas that year were radically different from what they had been before. Shauni and Shaila had always been my biological sisters. Now they were my sisters in Christ as well. My parents were initially taken aback by the change in their children's lives. They might have even felt a little betrayed, because this was not the teaching we grew up with. At the same time, they were supportive when they saw the transformation in our lives and were grateful for the good influence.

My conversion drastically changed my desires. On that Saturday when my world came crashing down on top of me, I was a mess because of how badly I wanted a cigarette. That desire and craving vanished instantly, at least for a while, once I became a Christian. My desire for Jesus was way stronger than my desire for a cigarette. Not until the end of March, about six months later, did I get back into smoking. Smoking is an incredibly difficult addiction to kick once its fangs are deeply lodged. Jesus had more work to do with me there.

Once I started getting serious accountability in my life and meeting every week with friends and mentors who sharpened me and pointed me to Christ, I began to experience real success in overcoming my cravings. By God's grace, I got to the point where I decided that I had no interest in cigarettes holding a place in my heart that rightfully belonged to the Lord. These days I've been smoke-free for a couple of years and am thankful for the victories the Lord has given me over this challenge. Through overcoming that addiction, I have been able to taste God's goodness in amazing ways.

The parties at my off-campus house continued, but I quickly grew sick of them. I was ready to move out. On a handful of occasions, I remember lying in bed in my room while a wild party raged downstairs. When I was fed up, I was fed up. I grabbed my pillow, packed a bag, and walked right through the party to my car. I drove to a friend's house and slept there for a few days. This happened several times.

My relationship with my roommate Thomas grew to a new level after I became a believer. He and I went to Bible studies together at 6:00 a.m. one day each week. That was wicked early. But we had to be done before my 7:30 classes started, so we went. The first couple of weeks were easy, but then it became more challenging because of my desire not to get out of bed. But we followed through. We went to Fellowship of Christian Athletes meetings together and hung out a lot, sharing what we were going through. My freshman year, Thomas and I had spent a lot of time together doing unwholesome things. A year later, we were both on a different path, spending our time together growing in Christ rather than pursuing sin.

I was experiencing a total revolution in my spiritual life. But at the same time I was still a world-class diver who was supposed to be working toward my goal of the 2012 Olympics. Honestly, in the early days after my conversion, my motivation to keep diving disappeared. I had no interest in going to practice. I was spending more and more time in church activities, and my passions revolved more around Jesus and his Word than the diving board and the pool. Though I never thought about retiring from the sport completely, I had lost the passion for it that I once had. Diving didn't fulfill me the way Jesus did.

I'm thankful the Lord in his grace provided me with exactly what I needed at that time. I began to meet with Brent Aucoin, a pastor at Faith Church who led the college ministry. Brent met with me weekly to counsel me and help me in my walk as a new believer. It was a train wreck at first because I had no idea of what being faithful meant. I was lazy. He would give me homework to do, and at our session the following week I wouldn't have it completed. I thought that homework was optional. He quickly informed me that, no, he'd given me that work for a reason, and he expected me to do it. He made it clear that I needed to be faithful with what I said I was going to do. What a concept!

In those sessions with Brent, he began teaching me that just because I was a Christian, and just because Jesus was my highest priority, that didn't give me license to slack off in the other areas of my life. That wasn't glorifying to

God, Brent said. He showed me that God had given me my ability to dive, and that was a platform for me to share the testimony of what God had done for me. I didn't understand it at the time, but I slowly began to learn that I could dive for a purpose.

That purpose, as Brent taught me, was to be a visible representation of an invisible God. As 2 Corinthians 5:20 says, I was now an ambassador for Christ, and God was making his appeal to others through me. When I was diving, when I was talking with friends, when I was doing an interview with the media, I was supposed to be the visible representative of God. I was supposed to show other people what God is like and what God's character is by how I conducted myself.

To be a visible representation of God, Brent showed me, I had to make the two main objectives in my life loving God and loving others. After I'd suffered so much emptiness for so long, after missing my purpose in life, God had redeemed me. No longer was I going to live for my own glorification. Now, my priority was bringing glory to God.

Once those lessons took root in my life, I started to pour my heart into diving practice again. I began working hard and not neglecting my responsibilities. It's easy for me to push my duties aside if I don't want to do them, but my growth in the Lord showed me that a man after God's heart does hard things. Like so many people, I fight a daily battle against living by my emotions and doing only what

I feel like doing. Brent's counsel showed me the danger of that and how it was inconsistent with Christianity.

That was a pivotal moment in my walk with the Lord. Though I was a Christian, I still didn't understand fully what living for God meant. My counseling with Brent revealed to me the purpose for which I was created. It gave me focus and a purpose for my diving. So I renewed my efforts and set my sights on the 2012 Olympics in London once again. But this time, I would not zealously chase a gold medal and worldly success to satisfy my selfish desires for glory. This time, I would be solely concerned with bringing glory to God through the way I treated my teammates and fellow competitors. This time, I would do my best and be content with whatever the results were, as long as I was doing everything to please the Lord by being a witness for him.

And this time, I would have someone new and special beside me to share the experience with.

CHAPTER 8

DATING WITH
A PURPOSE

I met Sonnie Brand in November 2009, just a couple of months after my conversion. A friend of mine from church and his girlfriend thought Sonnie and I would be a good match. At this point, the only dating that I knew was the worldly, recreational kind of dating. I had some occasional relationships before Sonnie that were all based on surface-level things like looks and emotions. These relationships didn't honor God, and I knew nothing about what it meant to date with a purpose. So that was my point of reference.

But Sonnie. Wow. My first impression when I saw her

was that she was smoking hot. Blonde hair, blue eyes, an amazing smile, extremely fit, about five foot six and three inches shorter than me. Sonnie grew up in Lafayette, Indiana, in a Christian home with a father who is an electrical contractor and a stay-at-home mom. Though she had been part of a Bible-believing church throughout her childhood, Sonnie didn't come to faith in Christ until her freshman year of high school.

She had a series of bad relationships with guys, and it got to the point where she was sneaking around and lying to her parents. Eventually the Lord convicted her of that, and she committed her life to Christ. She spent her college years at Purdue as a double major in dietetics and nutrition and fitness and health. It was also a time of tremendous growth in her relationship with Jesus.

We originally met at a get-together with some friends to watch the Colts play football. There were a lot of people there, and my friend's girlfriend and her sister made it extremely awkward for Sonnie and me, so we didn't really talk much that night.

A few days later, I asked her out. On Facebook. Yes, not exactly the most manly thing to do. (In fact, it was pretty cowardly.) Guys, I'd advise you not to follow my example.

Despite my bumbling, however, Sonnie said yes, and we went out for coffee on our first date. Neither of us liked coffee very much then, so I'm not sure why we settled on that. I'm also not sure why I decided that wearing what I always wore, gym clothes, was a good idea. I showed up in a scrubby, sweaty outfit at a coffee shop that neither of us liked. Regardless, the thing that struck me about Sonnie was how easy it was to hold a conversation with her.

I wish I could say that the evening was the beginning of a fairy-tale romance that led us straight to the altar, but that's not the way it happened. It took some false starts, some breakups, some reconciliation, and a lot of growing up on my part before we finally made a go of it. I'm thankful that the Lord in his grace saw fit to overcome my immaturity and sinfulness to bless me with a wife in Sonnie. She is a treasure far greater than I deserve.

Not long after Sonnie and I started dating, Adam Soldati began to challenge me on my motivations for that relationship. I didn't really understand his question, "Why are you dating?" I didn't think it was an important question to ask. Adam was persistent, however, and kept encouraging me to think of my answer to that question. The easy answer was, "I'm dating this person because she is extremely beautiful, easy to talk to, and funny." But Adam helped me think through the question on a deeper level.

He wanted to help me realize that the reason for dating was to pursue marriage. I just saw dating as something fun. I had no interest in marriage at that point. Adam challenged me to not just date recreationally but with a purpose that honors God and the other person. He and I read books together and listened to sermons together about the topic, and my mind began to change. I now see recreational dating as similar to going to a grocery store, opening a bag of chips, eating some, then putting the bag back on the shelf for someone else. Too often we pursue dating relationships only for what we can get out of them, with no concern for the other person, or the other person's future spouse. The idea of dating with a purpose is a radical departure from the recreational dating that is so common.[1]

After some time, I embraced this new line of thinking with gusto and began approaching my relationship with Sonnie from a perspective not of simply having a good time with her, but of pursuing her with the ultimate goal of marriage. Unfortunately, that mature approach didn't last long. Around March, after we had dated for a few months, diving season was in full force and my schedule was intense. After the initial "honeymoon" stage of my relationship with Sonnie, I became more consumed with myself and my success. I somehow came to the conclusion that my relationship with Sonnie could hurt my diving. So, I began pushing her away. My old mind-set was back—the only thing I cared about was myself, and I had no concern for her feelings at all.

I can now see the selfishness and the sinfulness of my heart during this episode, and I can see that I had no business dating Sonnie at all. She had been walking faithfully with the Lord much longer than I had, and she deserved someone who was more mature in his walk with God.

Because I blindly considered Sonnie detrimental to my diving, I broke up with her, like an idiot. Yet after a couple of weeks we went back to flirting with each other and playing the dating game without putting a title on it. I was totally messing with her heart, making promises without any intention of committing to them. That behavior carried on into the fall of my junior year. I was walking more faithfully with the Lord by then, and we decided to get back together. I was still learning to control my emotions and not to be ruled by them. Because I was a new believer, my walk with Christ looked like a mountain range, with high highs and low lows. When I was on fire for the Lord, I was fully committed to Sonnie. I valued her godly character, and I loved talking to her about Jesus. But during my low times I would push her away.

Our second round of dating was still shaky. As the diving season geared up again, I began to focus my energies there rather than on my relationship with Sonnie. Finally we reached a breaking point. We sat down for a discussion with Adam and Kimiko and with Brent Aucoin and his wife, Janet. By the end of the evening, all of us were on the same page. The two couples pledged to be there for us to provide wisdom and accountability to Sonnie and me. It was a powerful thing to see two married couples who wanted to invest in a younger couple and walk with them through a dating relationship. I remember Janet telling us that dating was much more difficult than marriage.

Obviously marriage has its significant challenges, but for those who are in Christ, it's intended to be a permanent relationship. Once that permanence is established, you have to operate within that framework. Dating is different because you can always walk away when things get tough.

And that's what Sonnie did. Despite the help from our friends, I continued in my immaturity, treating her disrespectfully, not leading and encouraging her well, toying with her emotions, and failing to point her to Jesus adequately. After a few months, Sonnie was done with this fool that she was dating, and we called it quits for the second time.

The breakup was a lot harder this time around. About a week later, Sonnie called, wanting to talk about things. As I listened to her, I began to see how much my sin affected her. In fact, it may have been the first time I realized that my sin could have a detrimental effect not just on me but on others. I had sinned against Sonnie by playing with her heart. Without considering the implications, I had told Sonnie that I loved her and that I wanted to marry her. I was concerned only with myself and not with her feelings. It wasn't my place to keep telling her that, especially when there was no promise of that on her finger and there was no wedding in the works. Sonnie was an emotional wreck because of how flippantly and carelessly I had treated her, which made our second breakup so much more difficult.

She wanted nothing to do with me for the first couple

of months after we split, but eventually the flirting and playing resumed. In August 2011, however, for a period of time after the world championships (I won silver, but more on that later), I relapsed in a big way and looked nothing like Christ whatsoever. I went back to partying and living the way I had before Christ had changed my life. I was rebelling against the God I knew and who loved me, and I was a fool. I let my old mind-set creep in—I wanted to live by what I was feeling more than I wanted to be faithful in my walk with God.

But, as Scripture teaches, the Lord disciplines those he loves. In my hard-heartedness and rebellion, God did not allow me to continue down that path for long. A new teammate who loved Jesus confronted me, telling me that the newcomers on the swimming and diving team thought I was an alcoholic because of my actions during that week of rebellion.

"You claim to be a believer, but your actions are totally inconsistent with the Christ you profess," she said. It took guts for her to tell me that. I was the star of the diving team, with all kinds of international success to my credit. I was an upperclassman, and she was a freshman. But she was being obedient to the Lord by confronting me the way she did, and I'm glad she was courageous and faithful enough to do so. That conversation was a wake-up call that spurred me to repentance.

Yet again, that repentance and a return to faithfulness to Christ sparked a renewed interest in Sonnie. From the time I met her, when I was being faithful to the Lord, she was immensely attractive to me. It's only when I strayed from the Lord that I lost interest. I think that says a lot about her Christlike character—or maybe my double-mindedness. You can decide.

My affections for Sonnie now back on, we continued flirting for a while until she put an end to those games in December 2011. "If you care about me at all, you'll stay away from me and quit playing with my heart," she told me. I wanted to ignore that request, but I knew that I needed to honor it. That began a silent period that lasted from December until the following April. We didn't flirt. We didn't talk. I stayed away.

Around that time, I moved in with trusted church members because I was still struggling with smoking and I was sick and tired of being enslaved to my sin. My roommate at the time smoked, so that wasn't an environment where I was going to thrive. I moved in with an older couple from church for the purposes of radical accountability. I even went so far as to turn over my finances to them, giving them all my money for them to distribute back to me as I needed it. That kept me from having the resources to buy cigarettes. I told them where I was going. I reported to them when I got home and told them I hadn't stopped at the gas station to buy cigarettes. I wanted to amputate my habitual sin, and this was what I needed to do for that to happen. It worked for a season, as I conquered some of my smoking demons, though they eventually returned.

This was probably the first time in my life when I really learned how to battle sin. As Christians, that's what we're called to do—put sin to death (Colossians 3:5).

Matt Chandler, pastor of the Village Church, says battling sin is like walking a lion on a leash.[2] The lion represents our sin; we often mistakenly think that we have tamed it when we've simply put it on a leash. We are deceiving ourselves. We may think we have controlled the lion, but in reality, the lion can turn and obliterate us anytime it wants to. If we're going to be successful in defeating sin, we can't just leash the lion; we have to kill it mercilessly. As Paul says in Colossians, "Put to death therefore what is earthly in you: sexual immorality, impurity, passion, evil desire, and covetousness, which is idolatry. On account of these the wrath of God is coming. In these you too once walked, when you were living in them. But now you must put them all away: anger, wrath, malice, slander, and obscene talk from your mouth" (3:5–8). Paul isn't messing around here with sin, and we shouldn't take our own sin lightly either. Sin is no joke, and it cannot be tamed. Put a bullet in its head and walk toward the cross. Sorry, was that too intense? Good. That's the point.

Too often we want to believe that we are powerless when it comes to the control sin has in our lives. And too often we're not willing to destroy that sin, because if we're honest, we like it too much to get rid of it completely. We want to keep it tucked away, pulling it out every so often, thinking we can control it. I lead a Bible study for college students, and I see this mind-set frequently—this sense of helplessness when it comes to sin.

Take pornography, for example. Porn is a destructive influence in the lives of countless men, both Christians and non-Christians, and it's a lie straight from the devil about what sex is and what it offers. I've seen many college students who are followers of Christ and who say they want to be free from the pull of pornography in their lives, but they aren't willing to fight it the way they should. They don't put accountability software on their phones or computers. They don't meet with Christian brothers on a regular basis for the purposes of accountability. Sometimes it takes radical action to kill the sin in our lives. That's what I did when I moved in with that Christian couple. If that's what it takes, then we should be willing to do it.

This period of silence with Sonnie showed me I needed to learn to protect her heart by not making promises I couldn't keep (and to show evidence that I could protect her). I acknowledged the fact that I had to stop playing this wishy-washy game with her affections. And it was a time of tremendous spiritual growth and maturity in my life. I learned what Jesus meant when he said that your yes should mean yes and your no should mean no (Matthew 5:37). I learned more about what it meant to be a godly man who was called to cherish, respect, honor, protect, and provide for a woman. By the spring, I was ready to get serious with Sonnie. And by "get serious," I mean that I was ready to commit myself to Sonnie and ask her to marry me.

Before we started dating again, I went to talk to her father to get his permission. I had done it each time we started dating, and it was totally my decision. I saw it as an opportunity for me to be more of a man and to show that I respected him and her. Sonnie was actually a bit surprised the first time. I think her dad was equally surprised. But I wanted him to be aware of what my intentions were, and I wanted him to know about what was going on in my relationship with his daughter.

He was undoubtedly and understandably bewildered when I approached him for the third time. But he gave his permission, and Sonnie was agreeable when I told her that I wanted to date her again with the intention of pursuing marriage. We had dated all of a couple of weeks when I approached Sonnie's father again, this time to ask his permission to marry her. He obviously had some concerns. We talked for more than an hour, but he ultimately gave his blessing. In May, about six weeks after we had resumed dating for the third time, I asked Sonnie to marry me. By God's grace, she said yes.

So I was newly engaged during the 2012 Olympic Trials, and Sonnie came to London with me for the 2012 Olympics. Our relationship was a point of immense curiosity for some of my fellow competitors. The British divers and Canadian divers, especially, were stunned at how quickly our relationship had progressed during that last stage, because the last time we had spoken, Sonnie and I were not dating. Then all of a sudden, here we were engaged. As I told them the story, I also explained to them our commitment to stay sexually pure until marriage.

"Like the Duggars?" one of them asked me. "Like the TV show?"

I'll never forget how floored they were by this concept, which was completely foreign to them. Sonnie and I wanted to honor the Lord in our decisions, and that included not having sex until we were married. That's the standard God sets forth in his Word. Sex is a beautiful gift from God, but it's one to be celebrated and expressed only within the boundaries of a biblical marriage. Don't get me wrong, nonbelievers do experience pleasure when it comes to sex, but they'll never be able to experience the fullness God intended for it without the bond of marriage and a saving relationship with him. The Bible is clear and unflinching about this (1 Corinthians 7), and Sonnie and I were committed to being obedient, believing that the Creator of life knows better than we do about how life works best for the greatest enjoyment.

It wasn't always easy. But I believe God gives grace to his people to allow them to be faithful to him, even when it's difficult. Maybe you're in a relationship now that is heading toward marriage, and you have made that commitment with your significant other. Stick with it! Waiting is worth it. Don't put yourself in a position where it's easy to give in to temptation and in the heat of the moment find yourself making a decision that is sinful and dishonoring to Christ. Find some people you respect at your church and ask them to keep you accountable.

Maybe you're not in any kind of relationship, but you hope to be one day. Make that commitment to sexual purity nonnegotiable up front. Don't pursue a relationship with someone who doesn't share your convictions, and be willing to walk away from someone who tries to pressure you into compromising.

Maybe you're in a relationship and you've already compromised and succumbed to sexual temptation. Or maybe you have in a past relationship. You are never beyond hope or redemption. As the apostle John wrote in his first letter, "My little children, I am writing these things to you so that you may not sin. But if anyone does sin, we have an advocate with the Father, Jesus Christ the righteous" (1 John 2:1). Confess your failures to the Lord and turn to him in repentance and faith, and he will forgive you. Jesus Christ is the righteous one—the only person who has ever lived who was completely righteous. His blood covers a multitude of sins, including sexual ones. So don't despair; look to Christ for the forgiveness he will quickly and willingly offer, and make a renewed pledge to follow him faithfully.

Sonnie and I were married in October 2012, shortly after returning home from the Olympics. She is a treasure beyond value to me. Having her with me in London during one of the most memorable moments of my life was a tremendous blessing from God (that story is coming). A greater blessing still is the fact that I get to spend the rest of my life with her. She truly is a gift that I don't deserve, and I'm thankful that the Lord overcame my immaturity and repeated faltering to bring us together.

A future diver. I'm two years old and about to plunge into the pool, with my dad, Jim, waiting to catch me, and my sister Shauni awaiting her turn.

Swimming with my dad in Lubbock, Texas, in 1994.

With my sisters Shauni (center) and Shaila (right) at our home in Lubbock in 1993, when I was four years old.

My parents, Jim and Sheilagh, were married in Japan in 1981 when they were stationed overseas. Eleven years later, they held an "official" wedding with family and friends. This is our family at the event on April 15, 1992.

With my sisters Shauni (left) and Shaila (right)
in 1998 in Noblesville, Indiana.

My dad and me in 2008 after the Olympic
Trials, when I qualified for my first Olympics.

The Boudia family (without me) in
Beijing during the 2008 Olympics.

The Opening Ceremony in Beijing in 2008, along with diving teammates
(from left) Thomas Finchum, Jevon Tarantino, and Chris Colwill.

Shauni (left) and Shaila (right) with me
at a party in February 2009 at Purdue.

Kimiko (left) and Adam Soldati (my Purdue diving coach) with me
during the 2009 NCAA Championships in College Station, Texas.

The Boudia family at my parents' home in
Noblesville, Indiana, on Easter Sunday 2012.

Inspire a generation

Ω OMEGA

MEN'S 10M PLATFORM FINAL RESULTS

1	BOUDIA DAVID	USA	568.65
2	QIU BO	CHN	566.85
3	DALEY THOMAS	GBR	556.95
4	MINIBAEV VICTOR	RUS	527.80
5	GUERRA J.	CUB	527.70
6	LIN YUE	CHN	527.30

The final scores of the 10-meter platform competition during the 2012 Olympics in London. My first gold medal. It was one of the most thrilling finishes ever in the event.

With my sisters Shauni (left) and Shaila (right) after
I won a bronze medal in synchro in the 2012 Olympics.

Shaila, Sonnie, Grammy Campbell, and Shauni
celebrating my bronze medal in London.

Photo courtesy of David Mason, ISPhotographic

With Sonnie on the evening of our wedding,
October 12, 2012, in Indianapolis.

With Sonnie, Shaila, and Shauni
at my parents' home, Christmas 2012.

With Sonnie on a training trip to Hawaii in 2013.

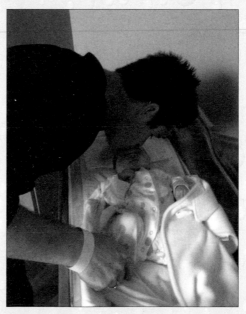

Kissing my newborn daughter, Koda,
on September 11, 2014, one day after her birth.

Photo courtesy of Paul Sadler/Sadler Images

A twisting dive at the Purdue pool in West Lafayette, Indiana.

CHAPTER 9

FIGHTING FOR VICTORY

After I became a Christian in fall 2009, diving took on a new life for me. Though I originally struggled with the desire to continue diving, as I've already explained, I eventually got back into my routine and my love for the sport. I came to enjoy diving more for the experience of it, with Christ now as the center of my life. I focused on things other than just winning and feeding my own ego.

This new attitude was put to the test in spring 2010, my sophomore year at Purdue. Though I had been dominant in regular meets all season long, I lost to a teammate in the Big 10 Diving Championship that year. I wasn't at the top of my game, and he dove better than I did that day. That was a situation I wasn't used to. It showed me I wasn't invincible. It also showed me how important it was not to keep my identity wrapped up in my success in the sport but to remind myself that my value and worth rested in Christ—not what I did in the pool. Diving was something that I *did*. It was not who I *was*, and it didn't define me. I'm not defined by my success or my failure but by who I am in Christ.

The rest of my collegiate career at Purdue was immensely successful. I turned professional after my junior year, so I only competed collegiately for three years. Still, I won six NCAA titles. I was the Big 10 Male Athlete of the Year and the Purdue Male Athlete of the Year in 2011. It was a great experience, but college success wasn't my goal. My goal was London and the 2012 Olympics.

I had accomplished pretty much everything I wanted to at the college level, and turning professional allowed me to get sponsors, make public appearances, and support myself financially. I remained at Purdue as a student. The university supported my decision and so did Adam Soldati, which meant a lot and affirmed to me that I'd made the right choice. It also showed me that Purdue was more than just about athletics. It was about preparing students for their post-college careers too.

Becoming a Christian radically changed how I approached my sport. I used to go into competitions focused solely on winning, and I would do whatever I had to do to make that happen. I didn't worry about how I treated people. I was focused only on myself. Now, however, I went into competitions with an entirely different purpose: loving God and loving others. I never did this perfectly, of course, but that was my objective.

Yes, the competition was important, and I wanted to win. But rather than focus on winning, I tried to focus on ways I could love my teammates and ways I could be different on the pool deck. That meant striking up conversations with people I didn't know, and, quite frankly, sometimes didn't want to talk to. But it got me outside of myself. My biggest attitude shift going into a competition (and in everyday life) was this: *I* was not the point. The whole competition, whether I succeeded or failed, was not about me. At the end of the day, I knew God was working all things out for my good, and he was doing what he needed to do to make me more like Jesus, no matter what the outcome of the competition was. Comprehending this took a huge burden away from me. When I experienced defeat and failure, I wasn't wrapped up in it. Ultimately, it was not important whether I was happy with my performance or not, because God was going to use either defeat or success to make me more like Jesus.

It was a rocky road sometimes. I experienced great spiritual highs and difficult lows. But I tried to learn as much as I could through the process. I'm immensely grateful that Adam, who remained my coach even after I finished competing for Purdue, was there to walk beside me the entire time. It was almost like he was holding my hand as if I were a child, because that's exactly what I was.

As I began getting more faithful and more serious about my walk, these competitions brought new challenges. I started drawing up a battle plan specifically for each competition. These plans would include my spiritual goals for how I would walk faithfully with the Lord, the Scripture verses I would memorize, the sermons I would listen to, what I would read during my devotions, and other ways I could direct my mind during competitions.

Why was this so important for me? Because competitions can be especially hazardous times in the life of a believer. Everything is all about the athlete. Organizers offer massages left and right. The food is all catered to my needs. I have refreshments. I have outfitting. I'm given everything and waited on hand and foot. In this environment, it's easy to become consumed with self. It's easy for me to start thinking that I'm hot stuff if I'm treated this way.

On top of that, competitions take me away from other believers. I'm away from my church and my circle of support. That separation made me realize how important the church is for me as a Christian. The Bible calls the church "the body of Christ," because no part of a body can live on its own (Romans 12:5). Likewise, this walk cannot be done alone. When I was away from my church, I found it easier to fall back into my old ways of thinking. I definitely missed the influence of my fellow brothers and sisters in Christ who could speak truth into my life.

In a sense, my diving competitions are still the height of spiritual warfare for me. Christians are always in a war against sin, but for me, that fight is more intense during competitions. If I don't fight my sin, it's going to annihilate me. That's what my battle plans are for. In the absence of my community, I map out who's going to hold me accountable for purity and who's going to hold me accountable for smoking. I plan it all out so I'm spiritually prepared going into competitions. I set spiritual goals as well as athletic goals.

This was a total transformation from my previous life. After my conversion in 2009, my perspective wasn't all about me and my success and trying to be a rich, famous stud. Instead, my perspective was based on bringing myself under the submission of Christ and seeing him glorified in my life.

Now, that's not to say that winning isn't important. Just because I had become a Christian and winning was no longer my top priority doesn't mean that I didn't pursue it. My competitive nature still burned within me. So while God commands me to love the Lord with all my heart, soul, mind, and strength, and while he commands me to love others around me (Mark 12:30–31), that's not at odds with a desire to win. And guess what? The Bible doesn't say God doesn't want me to win.

God doesn't call me to hold back from training hard or to hold back in a competition, because that's not pleasing to him. In fact, I think it's contradictory to what Paul wrote in 1 Corinthians 10:31: "So, whether you eat or drink, or whatever you do, do all to the glory of God." Christians follow the Lord by doing everything with excellence because God does all things with excellence. Being excellent is a character trait of God, so when we pursue it, we are modeling ourselves after him.

When I compete, I'm doing it for the glory of God. In any given competition I can be a finger pointing to God's goodness and a light shining on his faithfulness. I don't have to tear others down or do whatever it takes to win. If I choose to do it that way, that's disobedience and a perversion of what God requires of us. But to work hard and do my best, to love others around me, that brings honor to God when I'm on the platform.

In diving, the even-numbered years between Olympics are off years and are less important when it comes to competition. Those are the times to work on a new event or perfect new dives. Though Thomas Finchum and I had won silver in synchro in the 2009 world championships, I had a new synchro partner in 2010: Nick McCrory. The FINA

Diving World Cup that year was less than memorable for me, since we placed fourth as a pair and I failed to qualify for the finals individually. I was nursing a wrist injury and wasn't terribly disappointed about not making the finals. But those losses meant 2011 would be a critical time for me as a diver. The London Olympics loomed only a year away.

The World Aquatics Championships in Shanghai would be my first major test as a healthy professional. I needed to make my mark if I was going to establish myself as a gold-medal hopeful for the London games. I felt a lot of pressure going into the competition. The world championships in 2011 would be our first opportunity to qualify our country for the Olympics, and Nick and I adopted it as our mission: get the United States team qualified. We needed to place in the top three to do that.

We failed, finishing fifth, and we were devastated. At the same time, the failure helped us establish our relationship as new synchro partners. We learned how to endure failure together. Our disappointing performance showed us our athletic weaknesses and that we needed a stronger mental approach as a team. (We ended up qualifying the United States for the Olympics later at the world cup in February 2012.)

At that point USA Diving didn't have a medal at the world championships. Both Nick and I were competing individually, so we were the last hope for the American team. The individual competition in the 10-meter platform turned out better than the synchro competition had, and better even than I had hoped. I won silver, becoming the first US male diver in twenty-five years to medal in the world championships. The result boosted my confidence tremendously. It wasn't in a puffed-up, look-how-good-I-am way, as would have been the case only a couple of years before, but in the sense that I knew I had the ability to compete at the highest level and contend for a medal. The silver medal showed me that while I can't control the results, if I dive the best I can, I have the opportunity to get on the podium.

My silver medal at the world championships qualified the United States for the London Olympics. It didn't qualify me individually, though, so I still had to compete in June 2012 at our Olympic Trials for a spot on the Olympic team.

Nick McCrory and I were pretty far ahead of the rest of the field in terms of the difficulty of our dives, so we didn't have much to worry about as long as we performed the way we knew how to perform. I didn't have an advantage, but I knew if I dove the way I was capable of diving, nobody was going to take my spot from me. In 2008, I was just trying to get on the team before I could focus on winning in Beijing. In 2012, I wasn't explicitly focused on making the team. That was far from my goal. I wanted to compete well at the Olympic Trials to set myself up for success in London. And that's exactly what I did. Nick and I took first in the synchro competition, and I won the platform event to make it official. *London*, I thought, *here I come*.

CHAPTER 10

LONDON

Most people think the Olympics have begun when they sit down to watch the opening ceremony. For those of us competing in the Olympics, the journey begins much earlier. I qualified for London in June, and less than a month later—still a couple of weeks before the games opened—I was on my way to Rockville, Maryland, where I spent a few days training with the US diving team. I had waited four years to immerse myself in this journey. I was going to make the most of it.

It's difficult to describe the emotions that accompanied such a trip. The Olympics had been such a huge part of my life for so long. But when I met Jesus, he totally changed my desires, thoughts, and attitudes toward the games. I no longer saw them as a platform for myself—as a vehicle for me to get all that I wanted in the world. No, now my outlook was transformed and redeemed, and I saw the Olympics as an opportunity to display God's love to a lost and broken world. God's grace is the only explanation I have for the complete change in an entirely self-consumed pattern.

The local dive club in Rockville was incredibly gracious and hospitable, and I was honored by their kindness and care for us. We didn't deserve to be treated so well. The pool where we trained was a perfect spot—a simpler setting before heading to the ridiculously nice pool in London. The water didn't have sprayers under the diving board to break the surface and make the water easier to see as you're flipping and twisting through the air, so it pushed me to look for the water on my entries and stay tight. Those were the kinds of details that I needed to be working on before a competition anyway.

I had suffered from some tendonitis in my wrist that had caused me to miss some training time. But it felt much better after I arrived in Rockville. Adam and I were wise with the repetitions we did in the pool. Our goal was to train smart. We had already put in the work. I just needed to stay healthy, be relaxed, and strive to keep a Christ-centered perspective throughout my Olympic journey.

My second day in Rockville was extremely humbling. The diving team visited Walter Reed National Military

Medical Center in Bethesda, one of the nation's leading treatment centers for wounded soldiers. We witnessed firsthand the cost of keeping our country free. The brave men and women who fight for our freedom are the reason we have the privileges we enjoy in this country, and I was honored to meet some of these soldiers who had paid such a high price. It was a good reminder from God that I need to be thankful for how he has blessed our country. We don't deserve these freedoms, yet God has allowed us to live in a country where freedom is so fundamental that it is too often taken for granted.

When we arrived at the hospital, we signed autographs in the dining hall. The soldiers, it seemed, were so encouraged by us that they went through the greeting line, many of them in wheelchairs, and encouraged us to battle on while we were in London representing the USA. After signing autographs, the team broke into groups and visited different areas of the hospital. Cassidy Krug, Kristian Ipsen, and I went to the surgical floor, where most of the soldiers were nursing injuries from the war in the Middle East. They had been there anywhere from a month to three months.

We visited four different soldiers, all of whom were amputees. Talk about perspective. It made what we were about to do in London seem insignificant. All the little issues and complaints I had—the practices that didn't go how I wanted them to, the long days with the media— seemed pitiful compared to what these men were going through. I was thankful that God opened my eyes to see how un-Christlike I often am and how much I need him. It was heartbreaking to see the pain that these men were experiencing. Most of them appeared to be lost and confused. All I wanted to do was share true hope with them, but we were only there for a short time.

Even after that visit, it didn't take long for my heart and mind to go straight back to focusing on myself. It had been a long day already. After getting back from the hospital we went straight to a sports psychology session. I was tired, hungry, and deprived of sleep, and in that moment I missed an opportunity to bring glory to God and love my teammates. I joined in on the complaining. My actions indicated that I thought it was okay to have a pity party.

See how easy it is to justify sinful behavior? We all do it, and it's simple to think that we deserve things in our lives to go a certain way. On the bus ride over to the pool, the Lord convicted me of my sinful attitude through a conversation with Adam. Adam didn't call me out, but he is often open about his own struggles. As he talked to me that day, I made the connection to my own failures and shortcomings. I clung to God at that moment and took my thoughts captive to make them obedient to Christ.

After the complete change of heart from earlier in the day, I had a great practice. And I believe God poured out blessings upon me because I had been repentant. I didn't repent because of what I could get out of God, but because

I was truly broken. It can be natural to fall into the trap of thinking that if I repent, then I will get certain blessings. That's not proper motivation for repentance. And yet, God blesses those who do repent. It's mind-boggling to think about.

My practice earlier that morning had been sluggish as Nick McCrory and I worked on synchro. I held back on the takeoffs, and as a result, my entries were weak. I didn't have a lot of control or see the water clearly because I was tentative on the takeoff. Again, the absence of sprayers on the water made it hard to determine where I was in the air. It was almost as if I were diving with a blindfold on.

But the practice that night was much better. I made sure I was jumping strong. On my back dive, I focused on having my knees in front. On fronts, I got my arms through a little faster on my takeoff to help me generate more rotation, which helped my distance and form. In diving, everything stems from the takeoff. My front take-offs were great, and my reverses, or gainers, weren't bad. The first gainer, I was anxious on the platform and got dizzy. That affected my entry—badly! On the second one, though, I stood confidently, made sure I dropped my knees with fast arms through, and focused on seeing my toes on the come-out.

That's a lot of technical talk and diving jargon, I know. But hopefully it gives you a little idea of the kinds of things I was thinking about and working on as I went through my practice routines. Each dive was different, and I had to watch for different cues with each one. If I didn't, if I missed even one dive and didn't execute it well, there would be little or no chance of seeing the Olympic podium.

The next day we had an incredible evening at our Olympic team send-off in Germantown, Maryland. We went straight to the event after our practice at the pool. Hundreds of fans from all over met us in Germantown to send us off to London. The line to get in the door wrapped around the building. It was crazy to see so much love and excitement for us. People swarmed us, wanting pictures and autographs. It was definitely a taste of what it's like to be famous, and I was reminded about the changes that the Lord had made in my life.

Four years ago, this kind of attention was exactly what I was living for. I wasn't alone in that quest; it seems fame and fortune is an alluring call for many people. We think being famous will solve all our problems, when in fact it often causes more. As I stood there and observed my teammates, and as I responded to request after request for autographs, I started to get annoyed by how much people were asking of me. I started complaining to my teammates, because it was a lot—maybe a thousand autographs in a couple of hours. We think being famous is glorious, but we forget everything that comes along with the job.

This shows the futility that comes with achieving what we think we want. Anything less than knowing God and living for him doesn't fulfill and doesn't satisfy. It wasn't meant to. I thought I wanted to be famous, but when I encountered the costs of even a small dose of that fame, I had second thoughts. I complained in that moment because I had lost sight of my purpose. No wonder I didn't have joy. I was making the experience about me rather than loving God and loving others. I was missing the joy that comes from having an impact on someone's life. As I've grown in my faith, I realize now that the greatest joy comes from the self-sacrifice of loving others and being a blessing to them.

These autograph sessions can make your mind wander easily because you're continually focusing on yourself. It's a huge trap. I had to snap out of it and preach to myself constantly throughout the night, reminding myself that my circumstances were an opportunity to give God glory. He was continuing to build a platform for himself, and I needed to be thankful for the plan he was putting in place. Not only that but I needed to be a good witness to my teammates. The moment they saw me complaining and getting annoyed was the moment my testimony of faith began to weaken. If I represent a good God, I need to be that visible representation of him all the time, not just when I feel like it.

On our last day in Rockville, Adam and I attended church at Covenant Life Church, where Joshua Harris was then the pastor. The worship was a perfect way to end my time in the United States before heading overseas. Joshua preached from Matthew about the incomparable faithfulness of God in Jesus, going back to the Old Testament to show how God's promises were revealed through Christ. After the service, Adam and I visited a bit with Joshua, thanking him for writing books like *Boy Meets Girl* and *I Kissed Dating Goodbye*. He prayed for both of us as we headed to London.

The flight to London was actually refreshing. I was sitting next to my teammate Chris Colwill in coach. A couple of flight attendants told us to let them know if we needed anything during the flight, so I figured I'd shoot for the moon.

"If there are a couple of seats open in business class, we'd love to move up there so we can sleep," I told them.

A few minutes later, they came back and told us they had two seats next to each other in business class that we could have if we signed the back of United Airlines' *Hemispheres* magazine for them.

No problem.

We slept the entire trip, so even though we arrived in London at 6:30 a.m., we felt rested. Upon our arrival we immediately went through processing. Officers scanned our luggage as we went through security and picked up our Olympic credentials. The credential tag that hangs on a lanyard around your neck is everything during the

Olympics. You don't go anywhere without it, because you have to scan in every place you go. Security is paramount.

Our processing complete, we boarded the bus to take us to the Olympic Village, where all the athletes were housed during the games. The village was beautiful; it had so much space and a layout that was a huge improvement over Beijing. Housing in the village was divided by country, so we weren't intermingling with athletes from other countries a whole lot in our living arrangements. Each country had its own set of apartment buildings. In each suite was a living room, four or five bedrooms, and a couple of bathrooms. Sometimes athletes shared a bedroom with other athletes, and sometimes they had their own rooms. I shared a bedroom with Chris Colwill in London. I was also good friends with one of the Chinese divers, so I often hung out in his room in the Chinese complex, playing video games with him and his roommates.

I had to give my family a tour of the village via Skype. They were with me in London, but I missed the deadline to sign them up to visit me inside, so I had to show them all the amenities remotely. An athlete game room featured arcade games, video games, and giant, life-size versions of games like Jenga and Connect Four. It was like a playground for adults. Overkill? Maybe, but those games served the valuable purpose of getting athletes' minds off the competition and allowing them an opportunity to just enjoy hanging out with teammates or athletes from other countries.

Most of the high-profile Olympians like Michael Phelps, Hope Solo, Missy Franklin, and others stayed in the village with the rest of us. In London, Michael Phelps's balcony was right next to mine. I'd often see some of the more famous Olympians eating dinner in the cafeteria, waiting for buses, and spending time in the village like everyone else. The basketball players, with superstars like Kobe Bryant and LeBron James, didn't stay in the village, and about the only time we saw them was when we were getting ready for the opening ceremony. In Beijing in 2008, I was right in front of them. In London in 2012, I walked in right behind them. I actually had a conversation with Kobe in 2008 on the way to the ceremony. All the guys on the basketball team were friendly and always willing to interact with other athletes and have their photos taken, and they were cool about all of us being so excited to see them. Like the rest of us, they were proud to be representing their country.

In the village, you just scanned your credential at any vending machine and got whatever snack or drink you wanted. While athletes were separated by country in their apartments, that wasn't the case with the cafeteria. The dining hall was located in a separate building from the residential complexes, and mealtime was a free-for-all, with a huge cafeteria and food from pretty much every corner of the world.

Then there was the enormous McDonald's, a hair salon, a gymnasium, a place where you could ship packages—all of it located in the Olympic Village, where athletes were treated like royalty. Practically everything was free, including all the food and drinks you could possibly want. While the accommodations were nice, I had to remind myself that this atmosphere didn't have lasting value. The amenities, although cool, aren't that important in the grand scheme of things.

Those Skype chats with my family helped me to keep the Olympic world in perspective. Many times in the past I had felt too tired or anxious to speak with my family before big events, but that was a direct result of worshipping myself. Yes, rest is important, but it has its time and place. God had enabled me to see that a biblical man does hard things and puts others before himself, whether he wants to or not. A biblical man strives to keep God's two greatest commandments of loving the Lord with all his heart, soul, and mind, and loving others as he loves himself (Luke 10:27).

The building for the US athletes was next to the dining court and the bus stop for the venues—a perfect location. I shared an apartment with the four other male divers on the team and Adam. He wasn't the official Team USA coach, but he was my coach, which gave him credentials and allowed him to be there in an official Olympic capacity. Early in my time in London, I felt the Lord prompting me to be intentional and active in how I loved my teammates, to get the focus off myself and be proactive in finding small ways I could serve them.

It wasn't always easy; I often felt like some of my teammates avoided me. Part of that, I think, was because of my growth in the Lord. They saw the light in my life and didn't like being around it. I think another part was worry that they might offend me with the way they talked. All that meant that I had to look for ways to hang out with them. So I tried to do simple things like asking them if they wanted to go to the Olympic plaza or play games.

I was blown away by the way God was changing my desires at the Olympics. So many people were praying for me, and I could tell that God was answering their prayers. The Olympic Games used to be the main motivator in my life. I put it on the highest pedestal, and it meant the world to me. This time, I prayed that God would increase in my life and the world would decrease in its significance and allure. God answered those prayers. I knew I still occasionally used the Olympics as a tool to reach the old idols in my life, but I could see God's faithfulness in growing and maturing me in this journey.

The Olympics were not the most important thing in the world to me anymore. The old part of me kicked against the shrinking importance of the Olympics, whispering that it was the best thing in the world and the most important stage of my life. But that voice was drowned out by the growing volume of my heart's song to God. I saw his faithfulness in bringing me to this change, and it was unbelievable.

That's not to say that I didn't think the Olympics were cool. I definitely enjoyed them, and the Olympic atmosphere was incredibly special. My desire for the Lord and for spiritual things, however, was outpacing my love for temporary things like the Olympics. Remember how much I loved all the swag I got in China? We had the same type of setup in London, and I again came away with an entire wardrobe of clothes. This time, however, I gave a lot of my clothes away. Some of them I sold on eBay as a fundraiser for my church's college ministry. This time, I saw the opportunity for God to use me to provide blessings to others.

I was also getting my own blessings in London. One of the biggest was a guy named Brad Franklin. I got to know Brad while he was enrolled in a seminary program at my church. After he graduated, he moved to England and eventually landed in London, where he was serving as a pastor. Early in my time in London I connected with Brad. It was fun to see him again in that environment. It was another reminder to me of how precious the body of Christ is. When I'm away from home for so long, it's hard to maintain a strong sense of community. Yes, Adam was with me almost twenty-four hours a day, and I was grateful for his presence. But it was also nice to have someone else around—someone who was a brother in Christ and who wasn't living with me and coaching me. Brad provided me with some much-needed encouragement during the Olympics.

A couple of days after we got to London, we left for Sheffield, about three hours north, where our off-site Olympic training facility was located. While we were waiting for our train to Sheffield, we met some nice ladies from a company called the Wool Sak who had made little wool pillows for the US divers. I was thankful because they were extremely comfortable and came in handy for the train ride. We went through a security briefing after we arrived at the hotel, where we witnessed continued grand treatment by the citizens of Sheffield. The whole city, it seemed, was watching out for us. I had a strong practice that day and felt like everything was beginning to come together.

The next day was a disaster. It was one of those days when you have to throw your plans out the window and completely trust in God's sovereignty. I started to feel a little stuffy the night before, and my nose was runny, but I thought it might be allergies. I woke up on July 20, one week before the start of the Olympics, and felt awful. My head was pounding, my throat was sore, and my body felt completely drained. I tried to eat breakfast but couldn't. I took some medicine and went back to bed, missing my morning practice. I slept all morning, ate lunch, then slept all afternoon and missed my second practice and media day. My body was telling me to take care of it and rest.

A situation like that is always alarming. At first I was bitter because missing a day of training was not in the plan. But after the rest, I saw that it was exactly what I needed. I knew God was faithful and was more than enough. His plan was perfect, and it wasn't the end of the world for me to miss one training day. My skills and tools were in place, and all that I needed to do was pull them out at the right time. Though I could have been anxious about my circumstances, the Lord provided me with a peace and an understanding that my plan ultimately doesn't matter.

I felt a lot better after getting seventeen hours of sleep that day and night. Then I felt good enough to practice, which went okay—about the way I expected after being sick.

Another encouragement came from my teammate Brittany Viola. She was another believer on the team. She made little cards for everyone and told us that she had been dwelling on the word *hope*. One side of the cards explained what hope was (and wasn't), and on the back side was Romans 5:3–4: "Not only that, but we rejoice in our sufferings, knowing that suffering produces endurance, and endurance produces character, and character produces hope." Exactly what I needed to hear.

Nick and I returned from Sheffield to London a little earlier than most of our teammates because our synchro competition was early in the Olympic schedule. We wanted to spend some time training at the London Aquatics Centre to get used to the venue. As I had in Beijing, I participated in the opening ceremony that officially kicked off the games. But this time I kept it short. I walked around the track with Team USA during the parade of nations and then left so I could be more rested for my event. My experience during my second Olympics was completely different than it had been in Beijing. While it was still enjoyable, it wasn't nearly as memorable as my first Olympics. I was overwhelmed with the atmosphere in China. In London, I was focused on my mission and my goals: loving God, loving others, and diving to the best of my ability.

CHAPTER 11

4:6

After four years of waiting, my time had finally arrived. Nick and I woke up on Monday, July 30, and headed to the pool for our synchro competition. There were eight teams in the event. No preliminaries or semifinals, just six dives—all of which counted. Nick and I had spent hundreds of hours during the past few years training for this moment. All the conditioning, all the practicing, all the strategizing, all the planning, all the hoping, and all the preparation culminated in six dives.

Nick and I knew each other's weaknesses and strengths, and we knew how to compete together. That's important for a synchro team. A team is two different people coming together to work as one, similar to a marriage. I'm an extreme type A personality. I want to control everything. I wanted to control Nick, but I found out early on in our time together that I couldn't do that.

While I was always intense, Nick was laid back and at ease with everything. It drove me nuts at first. I had to learn that's just how Nick is. He might watch one or two of the other teams' dives, and that was okay. I preferred not to pay attention to the other divers. From Nick's perspective, I was probably putting way too much pressure on him. I'm sure on several occasions he wanted to tell me to calm down.

As we grew in our understanding of each other, we learned how we could encourage each other during our competitions. I learned what was helpful for him, and he learned what was helpful for me. Knowing what to expect from each other helped us to concentrate on our dives and not worry about what the other person was doing. We figured this out just in time for the London Olympics.

We would go into a back room after each dive, where I would distract myself from the competition with music and video games. When our turn came again, we'd get a quick word from our coach, climb the platform, dive, and repeat the routine. We did that six times. By the end of the competition, I knew we were in contention for a medal. Nick's face lit up after our last dive, quite a contrast to the look of defeat I remember seeing on Thomas Finchum's face in Beijing. I knew we had done well, but there were still teams that could overtake us.

As we returned to the back room after the last dive, I didn't know if we were going to place second, third, fourth, or anywhere near where we needed to be, so I tried to have a relaxed attitude about it. The competition ended with us winning the bronze. I was obviously over the moon with happiness, but I wasn't extremely emotional about it. Nick and I had medaled in competitions like this before, so in some ways I didn't see the Olympics as any different. Yes, I was excited, and I don't want to downplay that. I was just more restrained than I thought I'd be in my years of imagining myself on that podium.

Maybe that stemmed from the "what if" temptation that we all face when we succeed at something, but yet someone else does just a little better. What if we had turned in one stronger dive? What if the judges had scored us differently? Despite that temptation, I was learning to be content with whatever circumstance God allowed in my life. He always knew exactly what I needed, and I had faith that he would give me what I needed to make me more like Christ, even if it was last place.

Regardless, I had finally achieved my goal of winning an Olympic medal. The medal ceremony took place immediately after the competition. As one of the major sponsors, Nike had everything set out for us to wear during the ceremony: socks, shoes, pants, undershirt, jacket—everything. It was all there for us. We put on our required apparel, made our way through the mixed zone, and went straight to the medal ceremony. Unlike other competitions with maybe a thousand people in attendance, this time we stood on the podium with eighteen thousand people watching and cameras all over the place.

Nick and I were immensely pleased with the outcome, especially since the women's synchro team of Kelci Bryant and Abigail Johnston had won a silver medal the day before. Not only was the drought over for USA Diving but now we were two for two in diving events. We hoped the momentum would continue for the next several days.

The day after medaling in the synchro we did more interviews. It's nonstop media after you win an Olympic medal. Sometimes that gets old, answering the same questions again and again. It's always a battle for me to remember my purpose. But it does give me the opportunity and the platform to share my faith. That's a little harder to do when you're interviewing with a synchro partner, and you're trying to talk together as a team. I tried. The next day, after the media blitz, we returned to Sheffield and our off-site training facility. My individual event was still several days off, and going to Sheffield allowed us to get out of the intense Olympics atmosphere and relax a little more than we could have in London.

I think that was a helpful change from Beijing. Even though I spent much of my time in my room there, I was still in the middle of all the Olympic hoopla. Looking back on it, I don't think that helped me prepare as well as I could have. In Sheffield I could be around my family, and that was a big help for me. They helped me keep preaching to myself that the Olympics were not the most important thing in the world.

We typically trained once or twice a day in Sheffield. Physical therapy and massage therapy were mixed into the schedule as well, but the rest of the time I spent with my family, Adam, and my teammates, having lunch, playing Ping-Pong, discussing books we were reading, and generally enjoying togetherness. I returned to London after a few days and packed my bags again. My sisters and I were heading west of the city to stay with some diving family friends for a while.

The goal, again, was to get outside the Olympic Games and experience some normal, everyday life. Our friends picked us up at the train station and took us to their home, a beautiful estate in the English countryside. They cooked every meal for us and showed us extreme hospitality. My sisters and I loved staying there for a couple of days. I remember sitting on their couch watching the Olympics on TV and being flooded with childhood memories from when the Olympics first stoked this fire within me. It got me excited once again about being an Olympic competitor. I already had one medal. Now the time was drawing near for me to try my best to get another one.

The day finally came for the individual 10-meter plat-form event. The preliminaries were at night, so the crowd was large and the atmosphere was comparable to what you might expect in the finals. The one major difference is that the preliminaries are about three and a half hours long. The competition starts with thirty-two divers, each doing six dives. That's 192 dives during the course of the evening, so it takes a long time. I think the preliminaries are the hardest to compete in because the process takes so long, and it's nearly impossible to get into a good rhythm or routine the way you can in the finals. After the intro-duction of the athletes and the warm-up, you sit there for about thirty-five to forty minutes in between dives. By then, you have to warm up again.

It had been a long time since I'd been in a competition that lengthy, so that was one strike against me. Another strike was that I was actually too rested. That sounds strange, I know, but I was not used to feeling as fresh as I did. Because of that, I was jumping higher and finishing higher on my dives than I was used to. That's something you hope to experience a couple of days before competing because it allows you time to adapt to the change.

I also fell back into my old ways of thinking about my competitions: *I need to be at least fifth place going into the semifinals, because that will set me up to finish at least third there. That will set me up to win in the finals.* That kind of thinking left me in a bad place and focused way too much on results. I was playing out different scenarios in my head and worrying about things that I had no control over.

Three strikes. The prelims went horribly for me. I missed my fourth-round dive pretty badly. When you're competing, you arrange all six of your dives in a specific order. Normally, my first two and last two dives are my strongest and my middle two are not as consistent. My gainer three-and-a-half for my fourth dive was always hit-or-miss. Sometimes I would absolutely nail it, and sometimes I would fail miserably. Unfortunately, this time it was the latter.

I never considered the possibility that I wouldn't advance to the semifinals until I missed my last dive. "I guess my Olympics are over," I said to Adam after my final dive. I went back to my warm-up room, got dressed, and began collecting my things. My whole Olympic dream, I thought, was over.

Surprisingly, I wasn't that upset, because I had grown and matured in my perspective about diving and the Olympics. My life wasn't falling apart. I was resting in God's sovereignty and his plan for my life. My biggest concern was how I was going to face the media and explain my failure. I had already formulated a couple of different responses that wouldn't have been about myself. I was trying to think of ways I could honor God with my speech.

But then the catcher dropped the ball. In baseball, it's three strikes and you're out. If the catcher misses the third strike, however, you can run to first. If you make it before he throws you out, then you're safe. That's a good analogy for what happened to me. I had whiffed terribly in the prelims and should have been out. Imagine my relief, then, when I peeked around the corner from our warm-up area and saw on the scoreboard that I had actually finished eighteenth.

The top eighteen divers advance to the next round. By the slimmest of margins, I had made it. My Olympic dream was still alive. My preliminary score of 439.15 was something that I would have scored when I was fifteen or sixteen years old. Not good at all. But the scores in the semifinals would start fresh, so it didn't matter one bit if I had finished first or last in the prelims. I had advanced, and that was all that mattered.

We knew going into prelims that we wouldn't have a lot of recovery time before the semifinals. The prelims ended late at night, and the semifinals were scheduled for the next morning. I thought to myself that I could either dwell on my poor performance in the prelims, or I could file it away, move past it, and focus on the next day. There was nothing I could do about what had happened, so I made a conscious decision to leave it in the past and look to the future. When I got up in the morning, I was going to have a fresh start. I was going to be ready to compete and do what I had spent four years preparing for.

After a short night, I went back to the London Aquatics Centre for the semis. My six dives were the same ones I'd done the night before. I just had to execute them better. The divers went in reverse order from how they finished in the prelims, so I was the first diver of that day. That's not the most ideal position in a subjective sport like diving, because judges often don't score the early divers as high. They want to leave a little bit of wiggle room in the scoring to accommodate great performances from the later divers. So, if my dive would normally have been a 9, they might score it as an 8 or 8.5 so that they can give the higher score to someone coming after me. But that's not something I could control, and I tried not to worry about it. Once the competition began, I had blinders on. I wasn't at the Olympic Games. I was just doing my six dives the way I knew how to do them.

The only thing I really paid attention to were my cues from Adam. When I say "cues," I mean little pieces of instruction that help me focus on specifics related to my dives. Each dive was different, and depending on what my struggle was with a certain dive, Adam would give me a cue to remind me about what's important. For example, my fourth dive, that sometimes-disastrous gainer three-and-a-half, was clearly the hardest dive for me to execute technically. It's the dive that caused me the most anxiety. Adam and I decided to turn Philippians 4:6 into a cue for that dive: "Do not be anxious about anything, but in everything by prayer and supplication with thanksgiving let your requests be made known to God."

So "4:6" became my cue for that dive. To this day, when it's time for that dive in my routine, Adam gives me the cue "4:6," and I recite that verse to myself as I climb to the platform and wait my turn to dive. Thinking about that verse, especially on that dive, helps me stay more relaxed, which is a key to my success in executing it. We actually use the 4:6 cue on several dives, because if I'm too amped up, my dives are going to suffer. Other cues remind me to get my arms through quickly or to fully finish my takeoff. It varies from dive to dive.

The difference between my performance in the prelims and the semis was colossal. For one, I was able to get into a good routine. My routine concerns where I camp out and what I'm doing between dives, what I do before I walk up to Adam to get my cues, what I do when I walk up the stairs. Small things like that really matter. I'm not superstitious and I don't think I have to rub my hands a certain way or put my socks on a certain way or I'm going to miss my dive. Some of my competitors are like that. One girl I knew had to bring a specific stuffed animal to every event. Another one had to paint her toenails a certain way. If they think it helps them, more power to them. That's just not how I operate. But getting into a rhythm is important for me, and it's a lot easier to do that with only eighteen divers as opposed to thirty-five.

The results showed the difference. I finished third in the semifinals, an enormous improvement over the prelims. I was back on track.

CHAPTER 12

GOLDEN MOMENT

My struggles the previous night helped remind me that God was sovereign, and that his plan was perfect. True, I didn't do so hot in the prelims, but maybe that was to get me to focus more on God than on myself. Talking to the media afterward helped me to process those kinds of thoughts and get my attitude where the Lord wanted it to be. I realized that I had been focused on results in the preliminaries, and my performance suffered for it.

After the semifinals concluded, I had only a few hours before the finals later that night, where the top twelve divers would be chasing the gold. We went back to the Olympic Village to try to rest, but it's hard to recuperate so quickly. I iced and got a massage to help with the physical preparation. But the spiritual preparation was more important. I spent most of the time between the semis and the finals with Adam, and he helped me get my thoughts centered on Christ. We played some Ping-Pong, and I took a nap before getting ready. As I did, an extreme bout of nervousness overwhelmed me. That was uncharacteristic. I'd been in high-level competitions before and had not struggled with nerves like this for a long time.

I texted Nick Lees, a close friend of mine who was a pastoral intern at my church. "I don't know why I'm so nervous," I told Nick. His response humbled and sobered me. "David, what is there to be nervous about?" he asked me. "God has already walked through this. He already knows what has happened in this event. What you get to do is be a vehicle for his glory. So go out there and do whatever it takes to glorify him."

Even now it gives me chills to think about those words, because they're true. God knew what was going to happen. It was already written down. My role was to reflect him and honor him. That truth provided better perspective as I headed into the finals. My nerves settled, and we returned to the pool for a night that would change my life, though I didn't know it at the time.

Nothing would change in the final line-up. Same six dives. Same exact order. In that sense, it wasn't anything different from what I had done in several previous meets. But this was an Olympic final, and anytime you go into a final, there's always a different atmosphere. The crowd is larger and louder. Your heart beats that much harder. You jump that much higher. You spin that much faster. I wasn't nervous, but I was excited.

My warm-up was terrible. I got out of the water when it was over and looked at Adam, knowing that it was quite possibly my worst warm-up ever. Despite that, I was ready. *Let's go do this thing*, I thought. *Let's go to the Olympic finals and put on a show.* I left the warm-up behind me and got into my rhythm once again.

My positioning couldn't have been better. Diving right before me was Tom Daley, the enormously popular teenage British diver competing in front of a hometown crowd. Tom was one of the poster boys for the entire 2012 Olympics. Like me, he struggled in the preliminaries before bouncing back in the semifinals, placing fourth, right behind me. Immediately after me on the dive list were the two Chinese divers, Qiu Bo and Lin Yue, who were expected to compete for medals. The Chinese have dominated men's diving for years, so much that divers from pretty much every other country root for any country but them in competitions. We have nothing against them personally; they're outstanding divers. They're just so good that the rest of us have grown weary of them beating us.

While that positioning was challenging, and while it's

not easy to have eighteen thousand people cheering against you, I love that kind of pressure. I thrive on it. I'd think, *Tom's shooting for 10s on a dive, so I'm going to get up there immediately afterward and outdo him.* I think that's what all elite athletes crave: top-level competition from opponents who push you to do your best.

I was preparing for my first dive after Tom, going through my routine, looking at Adam the way I do before takeoff every time. I threw my towel down and stepped toward the edge of the platform when I saw Tom's coach waving me off. *What the heck is going on?* I thought. I stepped back while he walked around the platform to talk to an official. This kind of disruption can really mess up your rhythm if you're not careful. Instead of freaking out, though, I simply reset. I walked down the stairs and stood on the 5-meter platform to await the outcome of this conversation. Kimiko was sitting nearby, and we caught each other's eye, which helped to relieve the pressure and distraction for me.

Tom's coach thought Tom should get a re-dive because he was distracted by camera flashes during his first attempt. Re-dives are not common, but the judges granted the request. That decision was not something I could control, so I brushed it off. *Let him do the dive*, I thought. *I'm going to get ready for my own.*

Starting off well sets the stage for the rest of the competition. And this one started off well for me. I nailed my first dive, probably the best I've ever done it, posting a score of 97.20 that tied me with Germany's Martin Wolfram for first place after the round. From that point on, my adrenaline was pumping and I was amped up. You can't really explain when you get in the zone or how you get there. Everything just seems to work out perfectly. And that's what I experienced in the finals.

After hitting the water on my first attempt, I got into my routine and followed it the rest of the way. I connected with Adam to get any corrections or suggestions. Then I ran past the area where the athletes and coaches sat on the pool deck. My entire team cheered me on as I jogged by. I then walked into my warm-up area, a separate room off the pool deck, and put on my headphones, drowning out the boisterous noise of the crowd with the sounds of Lecrae's album *Rehab.* I sat there and played a game called Tiny Wings on my phone. I peeked out at the scoreboard every so often so I knew when it was my turn to dive again.

When there were four or five divers left ahead of me, I began to get prepared. I turned off my music, put my phone down, warmed up by shaking out my legs and stretching, and headed back to the pool deck. Adam gave me my cues for the next dive. I climbed the platform and waited for my turn to hurl myself off a three-story building into the water. That process repeated itself six times during the competition.

My second dive dipped a little from my first one,

dropping me to third place. I annihilated my third dive. A score of 99.9 (which ended up being the third-best dive in the entire competition) moved me back into first. Though I wasn't watching the scoreboard to see where I placed, I knew I was diving well. And I knew that when I dive the best that I can, I have a good chance of getting on the podium.

My fourth dive was the one that was so shaky in the prelims. In the back of my mind I thought, *What if I miss this dive again?* But this was a great opportunity for me, as a follower of Christ and an athlete, to speak truth into thoughts like that. I always run to 2 Corinthians 10:5 when I feel my thoughts drifting toward doubt and worry: "We destroy arguments and every lofty opinion raised against the knowledge of God, and take every thought captive to obey Christ." Because my identity is found in Christ, I can take every thought captive and see if it is in line with what God would have me think in this type of situation. I examine it to see if it glorifies God. This time, I shut down my doubts about the fourth dive.

That night the dive was not as strong as my third dive, mostly because the degree of difficulty was not as high, but it was solid. Once I went in the water on that fourth dive, I felt weightless. I didn't have any worries about rounds five and six because I was comfortable and confident about those dives.

Despite my confidence, my fifth dive could have been

better. Tom Daley had gone before me and posted an amazing 97.2. After my scores were posted, I heard this enormous uproar from the crowd. They weren't cheering for me. They were cheering because after my score of 91.8, Tom had moved into the lead in an incredibly tight competition. Going into the last dive, Tom, with a total score of 466.2, was barely ahead of Qiu Bo and me, tied at 466.05.

What a finish! A three-way battle for the gold, with one dive left to go, and three divers separated by a miniscule 0.15 points. The London Aquatics Centre pulsated with energy. This was one of the most exciting and fascinating Olympic diving finals ever, and I was right in the middle of it.

My routine stayed the same before my sixth dive. Tom's final dive was amazing, but a lower degree of difficulty meant he didn't score as high as other divers. Of the twelve divers in the competition, his final dive was only the ninth best of that round. The door was wide open for me to take advantage. I stepped onto the edge of the diving platform, keeping my cues in mind. I don't remember taking off. I don't remember doing two and a half somersaults and two and a half twists. I only remember coming up out of the water and not caring where I finished. I had done the best six dives in a competition that I'd ever done. I honestly did not care about the outcome, because I knew, without a doubt, that I had done my absolute best.

I went straight to Adam and looked at the scoreboard,

but it was all a blur. I couldn't process what was happening in that moment. A score of 102.6 on my last dive had moved me into first place, with only Qiu Bo left to go. My teammates were screaming for me. The Canadian and Russian divers (the entire diving world, for that matter) were screaming for me.

"What place am I in?" I asked Adam.

"First," he said. "It's going to be close."

I watched Qiu Bo's dive, and it seemed that he went in the water slightly over (not completely vertical). But I had to wait for the scores to confirm that. When they came in, I looked at the scoreboard, and my name didn't switch. It was still at the top. I couldn't comprehend it, but I had won the gold medal. My lifelong dream had come true. I was an Olympic champion.

Adam came over, hugged me tightly, and prayed. He didn't pray because he was excited. He prayed for my safety because he knew what was going to come next. Rock-star status is thrust upon Olympic gold medalists immediately, and Adam knew that though I had just won an important battle by capturing the gold, another battle was looming on the horizon.

It took a while for the reality to hit me that I had won the gold. My teammates, many of them bawling, swarmed me on the pool deck. I went through the mixed zone with the media and was still dumbfounded by what had happened. I was straight-faced and shocked. A couple of

Canadian divers who were friends came up to me and said, "David, you just won the Olympic Games. You're allowed to smile." That friendly chastisement snapped me back to reality.

I smiled. I had won a gold medal.

The medal ceremony followed. That was one of the most memorable experiences of my time at the Olympics. As I stood there, watching the American flag rising up and hearing the national anthem, I thought of how I had pictured this moment in my mind ever since I was a little boy. So many times, over and over again, I had envisioned what this exact moment would be like. And here it was actually happening. Nearby were the people I treasured most who had been supporting me my entire life. My parents. My sisters. And then the new relationships, the people who had played such a pivotal role during the last four years. Adam and Kimiko. Sonnie. My teammates and friends.

A sense of immense gratitude overwhelmed me, and the emotion of the moment overpowered me. I never wanted to be the guy who cried at the Olympics, but I had to fight back the tears. My heart was full. Not because I had won a gold medal. Yes, that was thrilling and the culmination of all I had worked and sacrificed for. But more than that, my heart was full because I realized how different my heart was. I had given up my laser focus on winning a gold medal in exchange for a more fulfilling and lasting focus on God, his Word, and his people. I came to the London Olympics with a goal of honoring God in my pursuit of the gold, more than just the pursuit of a medal itself.

And yet, God saw fit to give me the one thing that I had sought for so long. In his sovereignty, he had determined that the gold medal was what would make me more like Jesus. That's not to say that God will always give us what we want if we make him the priority in our lives. He's not a genie who's there to do our bidding if we simply say or do the right things. He may or he may not. He is God, and he is not obligated to do what we think he should.

For some, coming to Christ might result in losing a job or important relationships. It might mean any number of difficulties or hardships. The Bible tells us that Christians will suffer for the sake of Christ, so don't expect life always to be easy if you're faithful in following the Lord. Yet he's faithful to us through our struggles, even if they never go away. For me, God gave me what I wanted to show me what I needed. What I needed, more than anything else, was him. And the gold medal would clearly reveal that to me in the days ahead. It was both a blessing and a trial.

No matter what happens, God is a gracious, loving father who delights in doing good things for his people. We sometimes have this faulty notion that God is really out to get us or enjoys putting us through fiery trials. We imagine him sitting there, waiting for us to mess up so he can zap us and bring us back in line. We're tempted to think that we can earn God's favor if we just read our Bibles enough, pray enough, or live in a way that is holy or good enough. That's a faulty view of who God is. In reality, the Lord is kind and is quick to pour out blessings on those who love him, even if they come in ways we do not expect. God did not owe me a gold medal. Yet it delighted him to give it to me anyway. What an amazing God, who deserves our praise and our devotion. It's easy to say that when things go your way, but it's no less true when they don't. Even a defeat is an opportunity for me to say how good God is. This time, however, I got to praise him in victory.

The first few hours after the competition were a media whirlwind. I talked about what had just happened a thousand times, it seemed. After the medal ceremony I went through another mixed zone with TV stations. A press conference followed that. For the next couple of hours, the interviews came one right after another. I answered questions about what changed from the prelims to the finals. I answered questions about what it felt like to win a gold medal.

I finally got back to the village late that night and started packing. The closing ceremony was the next night, and my room looked like clothes had been vomited all over it. After such a long stay in London, packing was no fifteen-minute task. We had a team brunch the next morning with a little ring ceremony where USA Diving handed out Olympic rings. In the middle of it, the media relations representative came up and told me I needed to head home immediately, not waiting around until the next day, because the *Today Show* wanted to have me on. That's when it hit me how big a deal this was. Any plans I might have had for the next few days had just been changed, and it meant missing the closing ceremony.

After the brunch, Adam and I went outside and talked seriously for the first time since the night before. This was when it was going to get hard, he told me. I had done the training and knew how to battle spiritually during the competition, but I didn't know how to battle the onslaught of praise and accolades that was heading my way. I could tell Adam was legitimately fearful for my well-being in this. I knew it was a big deal because of how serious he was. The media would be repeatedly telling my story and presenting me as a hero. Fans would know who I was and want pictures and autographs. If you're not careful, you can start to believe your own press. That was a potential pitfall that could cause serious destruction to my life and my soul if I didn't guard against it.

To help, Adam asked Brent Aucoin from Faith Church in Lafayette if he could meet me in New York to provide spiritual support and counsel during my media tour. Brent dropped everything and came. What a huge blessing that was. For so long, my life had been a struggle to gain the praise of man. In an environment where everyone was giving me exactly that, Brent wanted to be there to help me fulfill what God was calling me to do.

I arrived in New York late at night and woke up about four o'clock the next morning to begin the media tour. I appeared on almost every morning talk show. I did satellite radio interviews. I did cable interviews. You name it, I probably did it. It went nonstop all day long. Get in the car, go to an interview, get back in the car, go to another interview. Over and over. I don't think I got back to my hotel room until about nine that night.

The biggest trap for me was believing the lie that I had accomplished all this myself—that I was the king of this triumph. That's a major danger for anyone who wins. It's easy to assume that it's all about you and you accomplish it on your own merits. So before every interview, Brent helped me get my mind right by coaching me spiritually. He wanted me to look every interviewer in the face, ask his or her name, and be intentional with my interactions. Treat them like human beings. It's easy to get into a routine where you do an interview and answer the questions, but don't take the time to truly see the person asking you the questions. He reminded me to be a visible representation of God by looking for ways that I could serve people at the media outlets I visited rather than just being served by them. I even got in the habit of giving people I encountered my gold medal and letting them put it around their necks. Doing that was a thrill to many, and I'm glad I could bless them in that way.

Once the media blitz ended, I returned home to West Lafayette. In some ways, I came home as the same David Boudia who had left a few weeks previously. I had a gold medal to my credit, which would prove to be another trial in the days ahead. In other ways, however, my life would never be the same again.

CHAPTER 13

PRESSING ON

The Boilermaker Aquatic Center on Purdue's campus is my home away from home. When I'm in town, I spend some time there almost every day except Sunday, just as I've done for years. Walk into the main entrance and through the lobby, and you see an enormous Olympic-sized pool with twenty lanes. Music plays over the speakers, but the splashing sounds from two dozen swimmers muffle it.

Past the swimming pool is the diving pool. The water in the diving pool is a much deeper blue than the water in the swimming pool due to the increased depth—seventeen feet. At the end of the diving pool is the collection of springboards and diving platforms: springboards at one meter and three meters and platforms at one meter, three meters, five meters, seven and a half meters, and ten meters. At the bottom of the pool is a big yellow Purdue *P* outlined in black.

The 10-meter platform is the highest vantage point in the building. I climb four flights of stairs to get up there. When I was in college, some adventurous (and insane) teammates of mine climbed up to the top curved rafter that's another seven or eight meters above the 10-meter platform. They shimmied across over the water and dropped into the pool.

My practice schedule and routine vary depending on whether it's peak diving season or not. During slow times, I spend more time doing dry-ground practice than actually practicing in the pool. The dry-ground practice area is on the second level of the aquatic center, with mats, ropes, and model platforms that mimic the feel of the real platforms. I go through a stretching routine, often bantering with younger Purdue divers. And let's face it: they're all younger. I'm the oldest on the US diving team in the 10-meter event. The average age for the entire diving team is probably twenty-three.

The younger divers like to give me a hard time. Maybe that's because I pick on them. It's my love language, and obviously it's all done with good intentions of building a relationship with them. I'm not on the Purdue team anymore, but I still work out with the team and use the facility for my training, since Purdue is recognized as one of a few performance training sites for diving by USA Diving and the United States Olympic Committee. Working there gives me extra accountability because it's easier to complete a workout or practice session with others there to offer encouragement. Or lighthearted sarcasm.

On the days I actually train in the pool, I stop at the 5-meter or 7.5-meter platforms to "model" my dives. Modeling is physically going through the motions of my upcoming dives. Most divers will model their dives like this during competitions, but not during practice. I do both. I want my practices to be as close to a competition-type atmosphere as they can be, so when it comes time to compete, I'm as familiar as possible with my routine. After modeling the dive, I stop, take a breath, then climb the rest of the way to the 10-meter platform. I focus on my cues, step to the edge of the platform, and take my plunge into the water below.

After the 2012 Olympics, I had to find a new synchro partner, which was somewhat of a challenge. Nick was finished with platform diving and focusing more on school, so I started the search for someone who knew the same dives we did. Enter Steele Johnson, my synchro partner since 2014, who is on the Purdue diving team and trains at the Boilermaker Aquatic Center as well. I believe having him here to train with on a regular basis gives us an advantage over other teams. In synchro diving, scores are based not just on how each diver does individually but how well the pair is synchronized. Because Steele and I work together regularly, our timing has become stronger, allowing us to work more on our individual dives.

I've known Steele since he was nine years old. He also grew up around Indianapolis and eventually moved to Noblesville. When I was a teenager, I picked Steele up and drove him to practice most days for several years. He remembers me during that time as an earring-wearing, loud-music listening, self-centered guy who exposed him to things that I definitely shouldn't have. He has seen the changes the Lord has made in my life, and he'll tell you that I'm at the opposite end of the spectrum from what I was as a teenager. He likes this version of me a lot more. It's taken some growth and maturity for me to get to the point where I am now, and I know I still have a lot of growing to do. The first few months after London showed me that clearly.

Winning a gold medal brings an instant and noticeable change to life. For so long I had chased a gold medal because of the fame and recognition that accompanied it. *How awesome it would be for people to know who I am*, I thought. *How great it would be for people to clamor over me and make a big deal out of me.*

I got a taste of that lifestyle upon returning home to West Lafayette. The celebrity status I had always wanted was mine. I was constantly recognized when I was out and about. When I went out to dinner anywhere in town, I'd get stopped at least once by someone who wanted to congratulate me or get my autograph or a picture.

I'd wanted that fame my whole life. Now that I had it, it was so much more difficult to know how to handle it. In fact, I wanted it to go away, and fast. It just goes to show how fickle our desires are, especially when we desire things that aren't designed to be fulfilling. It would have been easy for me to be short with those who were seeking my attention, but I strived to take to heart what Brent had taught me about intentionally looking for ways to serve others. I had to remind myself that people were excited to share their words of encouragement, so I could at least give them a little time, ask them their names, ask where they lived, and talk to them as one human being to another.

These encounters were, I came to see, an opportunity to live out my purpose of loving God and loving others. It was hard at first, and I didn't always succeed at showing a servant's heart, especially when I started to get e-mails from people I hadn't heard from in years and when people started asking more of me. "Will you come and talk to my daughter's soccer team?" "Will you come and give your testimony at my church?" It was a constant flow.

I don't like saying no to people, but that was something I had to do because I simply couldn't accommodate every request. I was grateful that so many people saw my story as inspirational and wanted me to share it, but I had to be wise and balanced in where I committed myself.

Several trips for different sponsors occupied a lot of my time. I spoke to Coca-Cola employees in Atlanta; TD Ameritrade employees in Chicago, New York, and Omaha; and Visa clients in Utah. Sonnie was sometimes able to go with me, which was great. The companies who invited me generously provided us with two hotel rooms.

When I got home from London, my first obligation was premarital counseling, which we began right away and continued for eight weeks. I thought I was handling all the fame fairly well, but our marriage counseling showed me otherwise. I had accomplished everything I had set out to achieve. The gold medal that was my lifelong goal was now a reality. I was getting ready to marry the woman I loved. It should have been a fairy-tale ending, with a life characterized by joy and bliss for years to come, right?

The problem was, my heart was growing hard and bitter. I think part of that came as a result of my celebrity status and the constant demand for my time. Though I tried to guard against that, and my pastors and friends provided accountability for the challenges I was facing, I still allowed bitterness to take root. I wanted some ease and comfort, and I wasn't getting that with my schedule. I was unintentionally keeping people at arm's length. My heart started to grow hard toward strangers, friends, Sonnie, and God.

Through counseling I learned a fundamental reality of the human heart. The human heart, when not being satisfied and filled up with God, will long to fill the emptiness with other things. The pressure of keeping up with my schedule was continuing to show me the problems in my heart. I worshipped (or longed for) the pleasure of ease. My bitterness came as a result of these frustrated desires of my heart.

The Scriptures teach in James 4 that the source of conflict and quarrels in our horizontal, earthly relationships is always a problem in our vertical relationship with God. We want something on this earth more than we want God. We believe these earthly pleasures and treasures bring lasting satisfaction. As we strive for them and then realize they do not deliver all that they promised, we can become angry, bitter, depressed, or anxious. In short, we do what we do because we want what we want in our hearts. My fruit of bitterness was rooted in my misplaced worship.

But my biggest issue was my continued belief in the lie I had started listening to as a child—that the gold medal would be all satisfying. Even though I was a Christian, and even though I had gone to the London Olympics with a proper perspective on my purpose, I began to lose sight of that in the days that followed. I began to get lazy in my thinking. I knew as a matter of fact that the gold medal wouldn't bring ultimate satisfaction, but I think a part of me still hoped that it would.

The Scriptures also teach that we become what we worship. For me, worshipping a hunk of metal resulted in me becoming cold and hard.

About the third week of our premarital counseling, the bitterness growing inside of me spilled over. I sat there in the counseling session with Sonnie and Nick Lees, who was leading the counseling, and I simply checked out. I was irritable and withdrawn. I wanted nothing to do with anyone whatsoever. I was turned off to everything, so much so that Nick spent the entire counseling session pleading to the Lord and with me for a changed heart and attitude. I started to reap what I had been sowing ever since the medal was put around my neck. In some sense, the gold medal was like the ring of power in *The Lord of the Rings* that would slowly but thoroughly corrupt its wearer. I was sowing a heart of ungratefulness, self-pity, laziness, and selfishness, and I was reaping the destruction that came along with it. It wasn't because I didn't want to get married. It was because I wasn't getting what I had thought the gold medal would supply: comfort, pleasure, and ease.

After all the pleading from Nick and Sonnie, I still didn't care. We left the counseling session in silence. I couldn't even look Sonnie in the eye. She had flashbacks to our dating relationship, when I had treated her poorly during diving season. I'm thankful the Lord quickly intervened. Later that night, he broke me of my hard-heartedness and selfishness. In tears and sorrow over my sin, I called Sonnie and Nick and asked for their forgiveness, which they graciously extended. I wasn't just broken over the fact that I had treated them horribly a few hours earlier but also because I had given the gold medal such a high priority. I had so much riding on the satisfaction it would bring that I had slowly pushed the eternally satisfying God out of my life. The same God who broke me from the chains of bondage I had to sin and myself. The same God who freed me to live a life not for myself but for him.

Looking back, the Olympics and the success I had there were an immense challenge and a threat to my spiritual well-being. The "me" monster inside me is constantly fed in that environment of fame and glory, and I let my guard down, thinking I was strong enough to battle it on my own without God's help in the days after the Olympics. Focusing so much on myself led once again to the attitude that had been so destructive in my life before God saved me. Though I have been redeemed, the old David, the one who loved David above anything else, still tries to surface when I don't choose to battle those desires. The old David showed up in a big way during this time in my life.

After tasting the fame and the celebrity following London, I can honestly say now that I don't wish that on anyone. It's terribly difficult. Acclaim from the world asks a lot in return. It can jade you and strip you of your desire for anything other than yourself. It can destroy you, as it almost did me, and it's not worth the price unless God sees fit to give it to you in order to show you that he is better. By God's grace, he brought me through those challenges and has used them to show me how good and gracious he truly is. I'm not perfect, and I still fail on a daily basis. I still see my need for a savior every day because of that. But I have faith that the Lord is making me more like himself.

A lot of that I credit to my church, Faith West in West Lafayette. There I am surrounded by brothers and sisters in Christ who do more than just attend church together on Sunday mornings. We are invested in each other's lives. We hold each other accountable. We ask difficult and probing questions of each other. We are growing together in Christ, and that kind of environment has been responsible for much of my growth.

At the same time, I'm not there simply to be blessed by other people. My role as a church member is to pour my life into service for others and to help build the kingdom of God through ministry. One of the ways Sonnie and I do this is by leading a college Bible study in our home each week and being involved in the church's ministries in other ways. We try to serve at every opportunity. Faith West is a huge part of our lives that goes beyond corporate worship on Sunday. If you are a follower of Christ, let me encourage you to find a church like Faith West—one that faithfully preaches the gospel, where church members invest heavily in each other, and where you grow in Christ through your involvement.

I can't overstate how important the church is to the believer. The Christian life is not just something you do solo. It's not just you and Jesus and nobody else. We need each other, and that is why God has established the church. As the body of Christ, we are to invest our efforts and energies in the church as we serve the Lord.

Things have settled down quite a bit for me since the London Olympics. Fame dies quickly. It's never long until the next big thing comes along and you are forgotten. Sonnie and I were married in October 2012 and went to the Bahamas for our honeymoon. Not long after returning, I did an eight-episode TV show called *Splash* on ABC, where celebrities like Kareem Abdul-Jabbar, Keshia Knight Pulliam, Ndamukong Suh, and others learned how to dive. That was also a challenge in my walk with God. I was constantly traveling to Los Angeles, far from my community of believers, in addition to fighting the temptation of chasing after riches. Again, though, the Lord saw fit to use that time to continue to conform me into the image of Christ.

Do you get the theme in the life of a person who is following Christ? God constantly uses our circumstances for good. He molds us to be more like his perfect, loving Son. Although we will never completely become like him, his attributes grow in us and teach us how to live a beautiful life for him.

An Olympic gold medal makes you more marketable, so I get invited to speak at a lot of corporate events and some faith-based events. I also have some sponsorships, so I do a lot of marketing and promotion with those companies. I give talks to their employees, participate in wellness campaigns, shoot commercials for their internal use, and all manner of things.

I also resumed my classes at Purdue. Though I had turned professional and wasn't diving as a Boilermaker anymore, I still wanted to finish my degree. I took a couple of classes a semester until I graduated in December 2013 with a degree in communication.

I'd never taken more than two or three weeks off from diving, but after London, I took a three-month break. Sometimes athletes are tempted to retire from their sport entirely after winning a gold medal, but I wasn't ready to be finished with diving yet. I was still young and still had the ability to compete. Plus, diving helped me provide for my family through the support of gracious sponsors.

Still, when I resumed workouts after my break, I found 2013 to be one of the hardest years in my diving career. I was traveling a lot, and I didn't have much time to practice. My drive to dive had faded. I'd reached the pinnacle of my sport. I started to feel like I was ready to retire. I spent much of 2013 evaluating whether I should continue or not. I didn't compete as much as I normally did because of outside engagements and my need for rest. I think I did two international competitions that year, the highlight of which was winning silver at the world championships in Barcelona.

Why am I still diving? What's the purpose of this? I struggled to answer those questions for a while. These were the same questions I struggled with when I first became a believer. But this time the struggle had a completely different meaning because I had accomplished my goals in the sport. Diving didn't feel enjoyable for a season, but I had to continue preaching to myself that God wasn't telling me to live by how I felt. If I lived by how I felt, I wouldn't be diving. But God calls men and women to do hard things, and this was one of them for me at that point. Diving was a means for me to support my wife and provide an income, so I needed to keep at it. As a husband, God's call on my life was for me to provide for my wife both financially and spiritually. If I were slacking in the pool, that would affect how well I could provide for her because current and potential sponsors would not see me as one of the best in the world.

I think that's something a lot of people can relate to, either in isolated chapters of their lives or for longer durations. Perhaps you find your work exceptionally fulfilling and can't imagine doing anything else. Great! Work like that is truly a gift from God. But maybe you're in a job right now that you don't particularly enjoy. You find it a challenge to head to work each day, and you wonder what the point of all your labors is. Sometimes we get the idea in our culture that we have to love our work or be passionate about it all the time. But you know what? This is connected to the issue of fulfillment that I struggled with for so long. Our work was never designed to provide us with the joy and satisfaction that we can find only in a relationship with Jesus. It may provide fleeting joy, but not lasting joy the way the Lord can. Sometimes work is hard. Sometimes it's drudgery.

I know because I've experienced the same thing. In times like these we need to remind ourselves that work is a blessing from God because it gives us a means to provide for ourselves and our loved ones. Even when it's difficult, we must remember that God has not promised us a life of ease or comfort. He has called us to be faithful, and that means being faithful in the jobs that he has given us. We may not like our circumstances, but that doesn't mean we check out. Sometimes I don't feel like practicing. We have to be guided not by how we feel but by what we know to be right. More important than our feelings is what Christ thinks, and how we can make our thoughts and actions glorify him.

Eventually I came to the end of that chapter of questioning with a greater devotion to my life as a diver. I resolved to train hard because slacking off would cost me down the road. If my intention was to use my God-given talent for diving as a means to provide for my family, then I needed to take it seriously and pursue excellence. If I'm not training or working hard, that laziness is going to catch up to me eventually and put my family at risk.

My work goes beyond just my obligation to take care of my family, though. God doesn't want me to be lazy. If I'm not working hard in the pool, then I'm not fulfilling my role to glorify him, whether I eat or drink, or whatever I do, as 1 Corinthians 10:31 says. Hard work and effort glorify the Lord, so that should be motivation enough for me to do my best.

Sonnie and I were still learning how to live life together, and we saw things in our marriage that we never could see while we were dating. Because of that, the first few months of marriage were a challenge. I don't know that our relationship is that much different from other newlyweds'. It just takes time to learn how to communicate with each other. I had fallen back into my smoking habit, and I even tried hiding that from Sonnie. She knew better, though, and that led to some quarrels. Finally, through an accountability relationship with my brother-in-law Matt Wilburn, I made steady progress in kicking my cigarette addiction.

Sonnie and I gradually matured in our relationship. I learned how to be a better leader. She also concentrated on growing in her role as a wife. That is why I love her so much—she is always looking for areas where she can grow in her walk with God. We were beginning to understand what a godly marriage looks like, and I couldn't picture my life without her. In late 2013, after a little more than a year of marriage, we found out that we were going to have a baby.

That revelation was life changing in countless ways, including giving me added motivation in the pool. Now I had to provide not just for Sonnie but for this little soul who was growing inside her. That, and my decision to add the 3-meter springboard to my diving repertoire, brought new life to my diving.

Adam and I decided to make the 3-meter addition because we noticed some holes in the event internationally. We thought an opening might exist for me to do well in competition. As an added benefit, it helped rejuvenate my interest in diving. Results in 2014 events, while important, weren't as important as they would be in 2015 in a year immediately preceding the Olympics. So we fooled around with 3-meter at a few events before deciding to scrap it and focus exclusively on the 10-meter for 2016 and the Olympics in Rio.

Our daughter Dakoda (Koda) was born in September 2014, and her presence has been a revelation on what it means to be a husband, father, and follower of Christ. Being a dad has taught me more than anything else that my life is not my own. I can see clearly how selfish I was before. Marriage demonstrated that to me, and fatherhood simply continued and intensified the lesson. The baby cries in the middle of the night, and I don't really want to wake up. But I have to because her life depends on it. Caring for her has taught me how to be a servant.

Her presence in our lives has shown me how gracious

God is in entrusting this child's life to us and how much a father can love his children. I can remember sobbing the night she was born, overwhelmed with amazement and gratitude that God would bless Sonnie and me with such a precious and delicate gift. "Every good gift and every perfect gift is from above," and Koda is truly one of God's gifts to us (James 1:17).

Leaving home for competitions is a lot harder now because I have a wife and a daughter. It makes me thankful for the technological advances that allow me to video chat with them daily when I'm gone, like we did when I was at the World Aquatics Championships in Russia in 2015. I won another silver medal, my third straight silver at the event. That outcome was pleasing, as it shows that I'm still right in the middle of things for Rio. As I look forward to 2016 and what I hope will be my third Olympics, I have a better awareness of my unique opportunities to be bold and to talk about how much God has changed my life.

The competitive fire that has burned within me since childhood is still there. I want to win every event I compete in, and Rio in 2016 will be no different. But as I age and mature, I gain a better understanding of what goes into that. I know I don't have control over my competitors and how well they dive, so the outcome is obviously uncertain. But if I can dive to my full potential, I hope to be one of the top contenders for a medal in Rio.

At the same time, the thought of another Olympics and

the potential aftermath intimidates me a little. I've walked through the challenges that came in the aftermath of a gold medal in London, and I know how easy it is to believe the lies that come with such exposure. I understand now, however, what to expect if God chooses to put me in the position to win gold again.

I hope you've encountered something in my story that connects to your life and your circumstances. Allow me to leave you with a few final encouragements that God has revealed to me and that have been beneficial to my walk:

1. **Don't live by how you feel, but by what you know to be true.** God's truth through Scripture gives us all the guidance we need for living godly lives. Your old self (before Christ) would live by how you felt. But if you've been made new in Christ, you don't have to live that way. You are free from that bondage. Sometimes our culture wants to preach that we should live by our emotions and do what feels good. While that may provide satisfaction for a moment, it ultimately leads to heartache and despair (Galatians 2:20).
2. **Take your thoughts captive.** Sin is the enemy. As followers of Christ, we are called to battle it valiantly and vigorously. Don't be passive in the war against

sin and resign yourself to the fact that you have no control over your thoughts. You do! God provides grace and will help you in the fight. Our obedience to Christ must be marked not just by how we act externally but by how we think inwardly. You don't have to give in to sinful thoughts. Take them captive to obey Christ (2 Corinthians 10:5).

3. **Be process oriented, not results oriented.** Remember the Olympic creed? The important thing is not the triumph but the fight. So many times in our lives, results are out of our hands and we are dependent on things we can't control for the outcomes we desire. Learning instead to focus on the process, the journey itself, allows us to focus our energies more on the things we can control. That, in turn, leads to greater fulfillment and more enjoyment as we go through life leaving our ultimate path in the Lord's hands (Psalm 37:5).

4. **Put your hope in the right place.** For the first several years of my life, I tried my utmost to find lasting satisfaction and joy in things that were never designed to provide them—in the creation rather than the Creator. I thought the Olympics and a gold medal were a surefire way for me to be happy for life. The result? Destruction, despair, and disillusionment. Fame is fleeting. Riches can vanish in an instant. Pursuing such temporary pleasures may provide

some momentary joy, but not joy in its fullest as God designed his people to have it. True joy on earth and eternal joy in heaven are found only in a relationship with Jesus Christ (Titus 3:1–7).

5. **All I have is Christ.** The most important decision you will ever make is whether to follow Jesus Christ, submitting to his lordship, turning from your sin and rebellion, and trusting in his sacrificial death on the cross as your only hope of salvation. You can take the gold medal away from me. You can take my health and my career. You can take my particular church. And as much as I love them, you can take my friends and my family. If all I have is Jesus, then Jesus is enough. It's a scary thought, yes, but true. He is worth every sacrifice you may have to make. He is worth every struggle in this life you may have. The Bible says that Jesus is the way, the truth, and the life, and that no one comes to the Father except through him (John 14:6). He is my only hope, and he is your only hope.

So what's after Rio in 2016 for me? I honestly don't know. I know that I can't keep diving competitively forever, but I can't tell when I'll officially have to call it quits for good. That uncertainty is difficult for me because I've always been a planner with clear goals and objectives to pursue. The nebulous future, in a way, makes me uneasy.

But while I may not know what my future holds, I do know the one who holds it. He is the same one who has been walking beside me all along, calling to me when I was rebelling against him, rescuing me from the depths of my sin, redeeming my purpose from the emptiness and hopelessness that once characterized it, and giving me a life that has eternal significance and meaning. The gold medal I chased and ultimately won will one day tarnish and fade. Jesus instructed us not to store up for ourselves treasures like that on earth, where moth and rust destroy. Instead, we are to lay up for ourselves treasures in heaven. For where our treasure is, there our hearts will be also (Matthew 6:20–21).

For much of my life, my heart was consumed with the earthly treasures that did not and could not satisfy the deepest longings of my soul. The ultimate satisfaction and joy in life is much greater than gold: it's found in those treasures in Christ that last forever.

ACKNOWLEDGMENTS

Many people have invested in me over the years and played a role in my successes and in shaping and forming who I am today. The more I start to name, the more I'll probably leave out, so let me take this opportunity to thank just a few who have been instrumental in my life and in making this book possible.

To my parents, thank you for sacrificing the finances, time, and energy it took to get me to and from practice and competition and for providing a loving home to grow up in.

To my spiritual parents, Adam and Kimiko, thank you for using your time to love me and to challenge me to love Jesus. God has used you to witness to so many people, and I am thankful you took the opportunity to share hope with me that September night in 2009. You sacrifice so much for the sake of Christ and are amazing examples of what it looks like to follow Christ.

ACKNOWLEDGMENTS

To my beautiful wife, Sonnie, you are simply amazing and precious to me. Thank you for loving me and being my partner in this walk of life together.

To the teams at Thomas Nelson and Wolgemuth and Associates, and to Sheryl Shade, thank you for your help in making this book come alive.

NOTES

Chapter 6: Chaos at College

1. William Meiners, "Diving In," *Purdue Alumnus*, July/August 2009, http://www.purduealumni.org/alumnus/2009_july_aug/.
2. Atlanta-based pastor Andy Stanley wrote a book about this called *The Principle of the Path* (Nashville: Thomas Nelson, 2013).

Chapter 8: Dating with a Purpose

1. Preachers like Voddie Baucham and Paul Washer were instrumental in changing my thinking about this topic.
2. Matt Chandler, "Put Sin to Death," February 27, 2014, http://www.thevillagechurch.net/the-village-blog/put-sin-to-death/.

ABOUT THE AUTHORS

David Boudia is an Olympic champion, a gold medalist at the 2012 London Olympics, and winner of multiple world championship medals. Winner of six NCAA national titles at Purdue University and winner of five medals in the 2012 FINA Diving World Series, Boudia was the first American male since 1986 to medal in the 10-meter platform at a world championship. He lives with his wife and daughter in West Lafayette, Indiana.

Tim Ellsworth is associate vice president for university communications at Union University in Jackson, Tennessee. He is the author of *Pujols: More Than the Game* and *God in the Whirlwind: Stories of Grace from the Tornado at Union University*. He and his wife, Sarah, have three children.